VIRGINIA.

—

OVERWHARTON PARISH REGISTER,

1720 to 1760.

—

OLD STAFFORD COUNTY.

—

WM. F. B

D0873328

CLEARFIELD

Originally published
Washington, D.C., 1899

Reprinted for
Clearfield Company, Inc. by
Genealogical Publishing Co., Inc.
Baltimore, Maryland
1994, 1995, 2000, 2003

International Standard Book Number: 0-8063-4592-6

Made in the United States of America

CONTENTS.

Historical Sketch of the County of Stafford,

AND

The Parish of Overwharton.

Views of Aquia Church, etc.

1856-1899.

PREFACE.

STAFFORD COUNTY, VIRGINIA.

THE County of Stafford and Parish of Overwharton derive their names from the corresponding ones in England. The County of Stafford was erected in 1666 out of Westmoreland, extending to the Blue Ridge Mountains, being the frontier county, and was about twenty-four miles in width south and west of the Potomac River. It was first represented in the House of Burgesses by Col. Henry Mees, June, 1666. (Henings Statutes, Vol. 2, p. 250,) he being allowed 130 lbs. of tobacco and a cask per day; traveling expenses at the rate of four days each way for his attendance as a member of the Assembly. If traveling by water, only 120 lbs. of tobacco per day. (Mercer's

Abridgment, p. 39.) The county first appears among the proceedings of the Assembly as a county in June, 1675, when with Rappahannock, Westmoreland and Northumberland, Stafford was exempted from erecting looms and weaves, in consideration of the newness of the soil and the consequent inability to maintain them; this being more conducive proof of its establishment as a county than the mere circumstance of its being represented in the Assembly, as by the law then existing, any county which would lay out 100 acres of land and people it with 100 tithable persons should be entitled to a representative in the Assembly, notwithstanding the Act limiting the number to two representatives for a county. (Hening, Vol. 2, pp. 238-9.)

This law was changed October, 1705, requiring 800 tithable persons necessary to erect a new County on the frontier. Stafford Court House was first built at Marlboro, on the Potomac, afterwards moved about 100 yards from the site of the present Court House, which was built in 1783—material, brick covered with stucco of mortar; main building 20x40, with a T wing 20x30; two acres of land for Court House and Prison deeded in 1783 by William Gerrard and William Fitzhugh. The number of voters in the County in 1899 was 1725; 1400 white and 325 colored. Population of the village of Stafford Court House is 25, all white.

There are but few records of old Stafford County to

be found in the vault of this ancient Court House until about 1699. Very many of those from 1699 to 1862 were either destroyed or stolen during the civil war. Those that remain are indexed so that examiners have no trouble in searching.

For the names of the Justices of the County from 1666 to 1860, see Vol. 2, p. 206, "Old Churches and Families," by Bishop Meade; from 1860 to 1899, we find, Edward Waller, 1860 to 1862; period of the war, '62 to '65————; N. W. Ford, 1865 to 1869; Charles Tankerly and John R. Evans, 1869; B. H. Hewitt, 1870. J. B. Jett, Judge of County Court, 1870 to 1874; J. B T. Suttle, 1874 to 1880; E. C. S. Hunter, 1880 to 1886; Charles H. Ashton, 1886 to 1898; R. H. L. Chichester, 1898 to 1899.—*Supplied by Mr. C. A. Bryan, Clerk of the Court.*

OVERWHARTON PARISH.

THIS Parish was co-extensive with Stafford County, covering a part of what was once Washington Parish, extending about eighty miles along the Potomac, in breadth about four and twenty miles, embracing within its territory what is now Prince William, Loudoun, Fairfax, Alexandria Counties and a part of Fauquier until 1730, when Prince William County was taken from Stafford, and Hamilton Parish was erected, succeeding Overwharton as the frontier parish. Of the early history of Overwharton Parish and its rectors, but little is known.

In 1724, there were 650 families and about 100 communicants. One church, Potomac (situated about nine miles south of the present Aquia Church), the brick walls of which were standing until torn down by the Federal army during the Civil War. It is, however, evident, from the number of white occupants of the soil within an area of ten miles, that there must have been frontier chapels of ease in the immediate locality of Potomac Church about 1675, if not a church. The Glebe Lands were within two miles of Potomac Church. The Rev. Dr. Scott was rector as early as 1710, and so continued until he died, April 1, 1738,

aged 52 years, 9 months, and 20 days; he was succeeded by Rev. John Moncure, a Scotch gentleman,
but of Huguenot descent, who acted as assistant or
curator to the Rev. Mr. Scott for a short time previous
to his death; Rev. Mr. Moncure continued as rector of
the Parish until his death, in 1764. Of the old Potomac Church, there are no vestry records known to ex-
ist. The earliest records of members of the vestry of
Overwharton Parish are those of Aquia Church, begin.
ning in 1757. This church was first built in 1751,
thirteen years after the death of Mr. Scott, and was
destroyed by fire in 1754, and rebuilt in 1757 upon
the original foundation, as charred remains are yet to
be found under the church, and about the foundation.

An inscription over the door states as follows:

"Built 1751; destroyed by fire 1754*; rebuilt 1757."
And upon a panel on the gallery appears the following:

"John MONCURE, *Minister*, 1757.

VESTRYMEN:

PETER HEDGMAN,	BENJAMIN STROTHER,
JOHN MERCER,	THOS. FITZHUGH,
JOHN LEE,	PETER DANIEL, *Warden*,
MAT DONIPHAN,	TRAVERS COOK, *Warden*,
HENRY TYLER,	JOHN FITZHUGH,
WILLIAM MOUNTJOY,	JOHN PEYTON."

*Meade says burned in 1751; in this he is in error as Mr. Pow-
hatan Moncure gives the record from the church door.

As to the successor of Mr. Moncure in this parish, it is probable that the Rev. Mr. Green took his place in 1764. In the years 1774 and 1776, the Rev. Clement Brooke was minister. After the Revolution, in the Convention of 1785, called for organizing the diocese and considering the question of a general confederation of Episcopalians throughout the Union, we find the Rev. Robert Buchan the minister of Overwharton parish, and the Rev. Mr. Thornton, of Brunswick parish, which had been taken from King George and given to Stafford when St. Paul's was taken from Stafford and given to King George. The lay delegates at that Convention were Mr. Charles Carter, representing Overwharton parish, and Mr. William Fitzhugh, of Chatham, representing Brunswick parish, and Mr. William Fitzhugh, of Chatham, representing Brunswick parish, which lay on the Rappahannock, and extended to Hanover parish in King George. In the year 1786, Mr. Fitzhugh again represented Brunswick parish; and this is the last notice we have of the Church in Stafford until some years after the revival of conventions. In the year 1819, the Rev. Thomas Allen took charge of this parish, preaching alternately at Dumfries and Aquia churches.* At a subsequent period the Rev. Mr. Prestman, gave all his energies to the work of its revival. The labors

---

*Mr. Allen took charge 1814; continued until 1823.—Pub.

of both were of some avail to preserve it from utter
extinction, but not to raise it to anything like pros-
perity. The Rev. Mr. Johnson also made some inef-
ectual efforts in its behalf as a missionary.

Old Aquia Church stands upon a high eminence,
not very far from the main road from Alexandria to
Fredericksburg. In 1838 it was a melancholy sight
to behold the vacant space around the house, which in
other days had been filled with horses and carriages
and footmen, now overgrown with trees and bushes,
the limbs of the green cedars not only casting their
shadows but resting their arms on the dingy walls and
thrusting them through the broken windows, thus
giving an air of pensiveness and gloom to the whole
scene. The very pathway up the commanding eminence on which it stood was filled with young trees,
while the arms of the older ones so embraced each
other over it that it was difficult to ascend. The
church has a noble exterior, being a high two-story
house, of the figure of the cross. On its top was an
observatory, which was reached by a flight of stairs
leading from the gallery, and from which the Potomac
and Rappahannock Rivers, which are not far distant
from each other, and much of the surrounding country,
might be seen.

After a visit made to the same church, about 1856,
Bishop Meade says:

" I should not have recognized the place or building. The trees, brushwood and rubbish had been cleared away. The light of heaven had been let in upon the once gloomy sanctuary. At the expense of eighteen hundred dollars (almost all of it contributed by the descendants of Mr. Moncure), the house had been repaired within, without and above. The dingy walls were painted white and looked new and fresh, and to me it appeared one of the best and most imposing temples in our land. The congregation was a good one. The descendants of Mr. Moncure, still bearing his name, formed a large portion."

The following is the view of the church subsequent to the late Civil War, supplied by Messrs. Lippincott & Co., being from the same plate as the one used in "Old Churches and Families of Virginia," by Bishop Meade, Vol. 2, pp. 197–206, to which publication I am indebted for a portion of this historical sketch.

About 1840 the church had fallen into decay and remained so, as stated by Bishop Meade, until about 1850, when the Rev. Henry Wall took charge as minister. He was succeeded about 1858 by the Rev. Mr. Mackenheimer, who serve until the Civil War, during which time the church was temporarily occupied by the Federal troops and, as a result was desecrated and defaced, for which a claim is now pending before Congress.

AQQUIA CHURCH, STAFFORD CO., VA.

Shortly after the war the church was again repaired, largely by the assistance of Rev. J. M. Meredith and Hon. Wm. S. Scott, of Pennsylvania, a descendant of Rev. Alexander Scott. Rev. Mr. Meredith then became rector, and in 1875 was succeeded by Rev. Mr. Appleton; in 1877 by Mr. Pruden; in 1878 Rev. Geo. M. Funsten; in 1884 by Rev. Thos. Carter Page, who remained until 1889. It was then vacant for two years, when Rev. John H. Birckhead became rector and remained until 1896. He was succeeded by the present incumbent, Rev. J. Howard Gibbons. The above dates are claimed to be nearly exact. Vestrymen before the war, not known, but the first vestry after was as follows:

Gen. FITZHUGH LEE	GEO. V. MONCURE,
WM. E. MONCURE, *Warden.*	HUGH ADIE,
R. C. L. MONCURE, *Warden.*	N. W. FORD,
POWHATAN MONCURE,	E. A. W. HORE,
Col. THOMAS WALLER,	BENJAMIN A. BELL.

The present vestry is as follows, viz:

JAS. ASHBY,	WALTER BOZZELL,
POWHATAN MONCURE,	*Sec'y and Treas*
HUGH ADIE,	E. D. MONCURE,
GEO. V. MONCURE, JR.,	FRANK BLACKBURN,
R. C. L. MONCURE, SR.,	R. MINOR MONCURE,
J. M. ASHBY,	WM. P. PATTERSON.
R. A. MONCURE,	

Number of families represented, not known. Present number of communicants, 80.

WM. F. BOOGHER.

To the courtesy of Mr. P. Moncure I am indebted for the following illustrations of the Exterior and Interior Views of this old historical Church, as it is at present.

EXTERIOR VIEW AQUIA CHURCH. 1899.

INTERIOR VIEW AQUIA CHURCH. 1899.

Overwharton Parish Register,

1720 to 1750.

A.

Aldrige, John. Married Annie Hamilton,
June 11, 1738

Abram, Mary. Married Walter Morgan Lewis,
August 27, 1738

Allen, William. Departed this life January 13, 1741

Asbee, Elizabeth. Daughter of Jean and John, born
July 9, 1742

Asbee, Stephen. Son of Robert and Mary, born
October 19, 1742

Atchison, Adam. Married Elizabeth Byram,
October 20, 1742

Allentrop, Jacob. Son of John and Annie, baptized
December 24, 1742

Allen, William. Married Bridget Withers,
February 15, 1743

Allen, John. Son of Archibald and Abigail, born
August 12, 1743

Allen, Margaret.   Departed this life September 1, 1743
Allen, James.   Son of William and Bridget, born
                                    January 2, 1744
Atchison, Mary.   Daughter of Adam and Betty, born
                                    April 11, 1744
Asbee, Stephen.   Son of Robert and Mary, died
                                    September 5, 1744
Asbee, Ann.   Daughter of Robert and Mary, born
                                    January 10, 1745
Ashby, Elias.   Married Winifred Million,
                                    September 4, 1745
Asberry, John.   Married Jean Boalin,
                                    February 25, 1745
Adams, George.   Died the first day of March, 1745
Angell, Samuel.   Married Ann Hornbuckle,
                                    August 14, 1745
Atchison, John.   Son of Adam and Elizabeth, born
                                    January 9, 1746
Asbee, William.   Son of Elias and Winifred, born
                                    April 23, 1746
Allen, Elizabeth.   Daughter of Bridget and William,
                                    born April 26, 1746
Allenthrop, Benjamin.   Married Elizabeth Fletcher,
                                    August 19, 1746
Angel, Jannett.   Born at William Black's,
                                    December 29, 1746

Asbee, Sarah. Daughter of Robert and Mary, born
January 17, 1747
Asbury, Ann. Daughter of Hannah and George, born
October 6, 1747
Asbury, Ann. Daughter of Hannah and George, died
February 5, 1748
Atchison, Lucy. Daughter of Adam and Elizabeth,
born December 26, 1747
Allenthrop, Sarah. Married William Price,
August 5, 1748
Asberry, Ann. Married John Wilson, August 16, 1748
Asbury, William. Married Jean Aukerum,
January 13, 1749
Aukerum, Jean. Married William Asbury,
January 13, 1749
Ashby, Fransisina. Daughter of Winifred and Elias,
born March 15, 1749
Ashby, Thomas. Son of Robert and Mary, born
March 5, 1749
Anglis, William. Son of Christopher, born
March 9, 1749
Adie, Martha. Wife of Hugh, died October 19, 1749
Aubury, Henry. Son of George and Hannah, born
February 10, 1750
Atchison, Rosinah. Daughter of Adam and Elizabeth,
born May 6, 1750

Angel, Margaret.   Daughter of Samuel and Ann, born
May 29, 1750

Ashby, Jess.   Son of Margaret, born May 20, 1750

Angell, John.   Married Milley Harvey, October 5, 1750

Adams, John.   Married Honora Carty,
September 23, 1750

Asbury, Thomas.   Married Martha Jennings,
December 1, 1751

Asbury, Mary.   Daughter of John and Jean, born
September 20, 1750

Adams, William.   Son of John and Honora, born
April 17, 1751

Ashby, Elisha.   Son of Elias and Winifred, born
December 26, 1751

Ashby, Thomas.   Married Mary Maccullough,
November 14, 1751

Ashby, Millie.   Daughter of Robert and Mary, born
September 11, 1751

Atchison, Jean.   Daughter of Adam and Elizabeth,
born April 13, 1752

Angel, Ann.   Daughter of Samuel and Ann, born
April 2, 1752

Asbee, Mary Ann.   Daughter of Thomas, born
July 30, 1752

Anderson, John.   Married Sarah Carney,
November 28, 1752

Angel, George.   Son of John and Mildred, born
                                October 20, 1752
Asbury, Ann Harris.   Daughter of Benjamin and Sarah,
                                born April 21, 1753
Asbury, Benjamin.   Son of John and Jean, born
                                July 20, 1753
Anderson, Baily.   Son of John and Sarah, born
                                November 13, 1753
Ashby, Wilmoth.   Daughter of Robert, Jr., born
                                October 28, 1753
Allenthrop, Margaret.   Married John Read,
                                March 5, 1754
Angel, Franky.   Daughter of Samuel and Ann, born
                                February 7, 1754
Asbrook, Nancy.   Daughter of Jane, born June 11, 1754
Angel, Frances.   Daughter of John and Mildred, born
                                August 18, 1754
Adie, William.   Married Elizabeth Parinder,
                                July 25, 1754
Asbury, Nelly.   Daughter of George and Hannah, born
                                June 13, 1754
Asbee, Elizabeth.   Wife of Robert, died
                                October 15, 1754
Allen, George.   Departed this life December 3, 1754
Asbee, Elizabeth.   Daughter of Mary and Thomas,
                                born November 3, 1754

Abbot, John.   Son of John, was born January 6, 1755
Asbury, William Boling.   Son of John and Jane, born
January 20, 1755
Asbury, Frances.   Wife of Benjamin, died
May 8, 1755
Asbury, Mary.   Daughter of George, died July 5, 1755
Ashby, John.   Married Sarah Maccullough,
February 26, 1756
Atchison, Nathanel.   Son of Adam and Elizabeth, born
February 1, 1756
Ashby, Catharine.   Married Isaac Murphy,
January 1, 1756
Ashby, John.   Son of John, was born June 6, 1756
Ashby, William.   Son of Robert, baptized
July 25, 1756
Anderson, Scarlet.   Son of John and Sarah, born
June 20, 1756
Abbot, Rachel.   Married Peter Knight,
December 19, 1756
Asbury, Eliza.   Daughter of Benjamin, born
December 23, 1756
Adie, Ann Fisher.   Daughter of William and Elizabeth,
born November 29, 1756
Abbot, George.   Son of John, was born May 11, 1757
Ashby, Hanknsson.   Son of Thomas and Mary, born
February 6, 1757

Asbury, Jeremiah.   Son of George and Hannah, born
June 21, 1757

Amely, Bridget.   Married Thomas Riddle,
February 5, 1758

Abbott, Ann.   Married Ephrine Knight,
February 12, 1758

Abbot, John.   Married Margaret Lyon,
January 15, 1758

Abbot, John.   Son of John, was baptized
January 6, 1758

Anderson, Lela.   Was baptized April 9, 1758

Ashby, Bailey.   Son of John and Sarah, born
November 22, 1858

B.

Bussel, Thomas.   Son of James and Martha, born
January 27, 1727

Brent, Innis.   Son of Charles and Hannah, born
July 24, 1727

Brent, Mary.   Daughter of Charles and Hannah, born
May 25, 1732

Brent, Charles.   Son of Charles and Hannah, born
June 11, 1735

Baker, Anne.   Daughter of Edward, born April 1, 1737

Brent, Jean.   Daughter of George and Catharine, born
April 10, 1738

Baker, Eleanor. Daughter of Edward, born
March 6, 1739

Brent, Susannah. Daughter of Benjamin and Mary,
born November 29, 1739

Brent, Hugh. Son of Charles and Hannah, born
November 3, 1739

Bethel, William. Married Jean Hurst,
December 26, 1739

Ball, William. Son of Edward and Sarah, born
January 14, 1740

Bethel, James. Son of Edward and Mary, born
January 27, 1740

Bethel, John. Son of Elizabeth, born January 24, 1740

Bridwell, Isaai. Married Abigail Green,
January 20, 1740

Baliwoel, Martha. Departed this life April 13, 1740

Bridwell, Elizabeth. Married Arron Garrison,
May 10, 1740

Barret, Ellen. Married Rev. Daniel McDonold,
July 26, 1740

Bridwell, Elizabeth. Daughter of John, died
October 1, 1740

Bridwell, William. Son of John and Lucy, born
October 19, 1740

Brent, George. Son of George and Catharine, born
October 23, 1740

Byrom, Sarah.   Daughter of Cuthbert and Sarah, born
November 14, 1740

Baker, Jean.   Daughter of Edward, born
December 29, 1740, and died January 21, 1741

Bethel, James.   Son of Edward, died January, 1741

Butler, Thomas.   Married Mary Mason, April 7, 1741

Ball, Caleb.   Son of John, died June 21, 1741

Bell, Thomas.   Married Mary Latham, June 25, 1741

Brown, Frances.   Daughter of Dr. Gustavus Brown, of
Charles County, Maryland.   Married the Rev.
John Moncure, Rector of this Parish,
June 18, 1741

Brooks, Matthew.   Married Mary Box,
August 23, 1741

Box, Mary.   Married Matthew Brooks,
August 23, 1741

Burton, Lettie.   Married Alexander Jefferies,
September 30, 1741

Burchel, Nanny.   Daughter of Charles and Margaret,
born October 12, 1741.

Botts, Elizabeth.   Daughter of Seth and Lib, born
October 3, 1741

Bethel, Peggy.   Daughter of William and Jean, born
November 30, 1741

Botts, Thomas.   Died at Robert Ashby's,
March 9, 1742

Brent, William.   Son of Charles and Hannah, born
May 19, 1742

Bannester, John.   Son of William, died March 20, 1742

Baker, Edward.   Son of Edward and Ann, born
January 4, 1742

Barber, James.   Son of John and Elizabeth, born
August 16, 1742

Brent, Captain William.   Died at Aquia,
August 17, 1742

Byram, Elizabeth.   Married Adam Atchison,
October 20, 1742

Berry, Lawrence.   Son of Sarah, born
December 23, 1742

Bazell, William.   Son of Hannah, born
January 13, 1743

Bridwell, Sarah.   Daughter of John, born
January 13, 1743

Byram, John.   Son of Cuthbert and Sarah, born
January 19, 1743

Baylis, John.   Son of Mulrain and Winifred, born
February 19, 1743

Brooks, Matthew.   Married Jean Jack, February, 1743

Bridwell, William.   Son of Abraham, died
April 5, 1743

Byram, John.   Son of Cuthbert and Sarah, died
March 20, 1743

Bridwell, Sarah. Daughter of Abigail, born
May 23, 1743

Boling, Edward. Married Mary Suddeth,
May 4, 1744

Bridwell, Isaac. Son of Abraham and Mary, born
June 17, 1743

Bell, John. Son of Thomas and Mary, born
July 2, 1743

Baylis, John. Son of Mulrain, died July 16, 1743

Byram, Liny. Married William Gough,
October 19, 1743

Butler, Thomas. Departed this life December 3, 1743

Barby, Joseph. Son of Thomas, baptized
March 18, 1744

Brent, Mary. Daughter of Benjamin and Mary, born
March 13, 1744

Botts, William. Son of Seth and Lib, born
April 16, 1744

Brent, George. Son of Charles and Hannah, born
June 7, 1744

Burchell, Charles. Son of Charles, born
July 10, 1744

Bethel, John. Son of Edward and Mary, born
June 23, 1744

Byram, Winifred. Daughter of Cuthbert and Sarah,
born September 26, 1744

Berry, Sarah.   Married John Ellis, September 30, 1744

Briand, Mary.   Married John Fling,

> December 31, 1744

Burris, William.   Son of Thomas and Mary, born

> December 19, 1744

Bridwell, John.   Son of Isaac and Abigail, born

> December 7, 1744

Bell, John.   Son of Thomas and Mary, died

> October 27, 1744

Bell, George.   Married Ann Hanson, April 15, 1745

Burchell, Charles.   Died at his home, March 25, 1745

Butler, Joseph.   Married Ann Carter,

> November 28, 1745

Butler, Margaret.   Married Alexander Nelson,

> February 21, 1745

Barbee, Mary.   Married William Cotney,

> February 24, 1745

Boalin, Jean.   Married John Asberry,

> February 25, 1745

Bridwell, Robert.   Married Elizabeth Jones.

> January 13, 1745

Baylis, Peggy.   Daughter of Mulrain, born

> February 2, 1745

Broderick, Sarah.   Married John Camon, July 8, 1745

Broderick, Christopher.   Married Sarah Hammet,

> December 19, 1744

Bridwell, Mary. Daughter of John and Lucy, born
June 19, 1745

Bassiet, Isaac. Married Mary Rhodes, May 18, 1745

Bell, Charity. Daughter of Thomas, born
October 20, 1745

Black, William. Married Ann Dent, October 17, 1745

Bethel, Mary. Married Joseph Lee,
November 14, 1745

Broderick, Mary. Daughter of Christopher and Sarah,
born October 20, 1745

Bell, Mary. Daughter of Ann, born January 7, 1746

Bridwell, Thomas. Son of Jacob and Elizabeth, born
January 21, 1746

Balls, John. Married Margaret Williams,
January 2, 1746

Burton, Priscilla. Daughter of William, born
January 17, 1746

Bridwell, Mary. Daughter of John and Lucy, died
February 22, 1746

Bannister, Henry. Son of Susannah, born
April 29, 1746

Bridwell, Mildred. Daughter of Samuel and Mary,
died March 23, 1746

Botts, Aaron. Son of Seth, born July 30, 1746

Boan, Elizabeth. Married Jacob Begoley,
August 4, 1746

Begoley, Jacob.   Married Elizabeth Boan,
August 4, 1746

Burchell, Margaret.   Married George Hinson,
December 29, 1746

Byram, Milley.   Daughter of Elizabeth, born
December 10, 1746

Baylis, John.   Died at his home, December 8, 1746

Bell, Elizabeth.   Daughter of Andrew and Mary,
October 26, 1746

Begoley, William Larien.   Son of Jacob and Elizabeth,
baptized November 1, 1746

Bolling, John.   Son of Edmund and Mary, born
September 14, 1746

Blackman, Hannah.   Married Joseph Noble,
September 7, 1746

Bridwell, William.   Son of Isaac and Abigal, born
February 10, 1747

Bryan, Lucy.   Daughter of Cuthbert, born
January 29, 1747

Battoo, James.   Married Winney Holiday,
February 12, 1747

Battoo, Mary.   Daughter of James and Winifred, born
April 29, 1747

Bussel, James.   Son of Winifred, born May 20, 1747

Bethel, Mary.   Daughter of Edward and Mary, born
July 23, 1747

Bridwell, Sarah. Daughter of Abraham, born

July 25, 1747

Baker, John. Married Rebecca Lunsford,

June 8, 1747

Baley, Simson. Married Elizabeth MacCarty,

December 24, 1747

Baylis, Winny. Daughter of John and Mary, born

November 1, 1747

Baylis, Mary. Married John Baylis, October 8, 1747

Baylis, John. Married Mary Baylis, October 8, 1747

Bell, Elizabeth. Daughter of George and Ann, born

January 31, 1748

Bussel, Hannah. Married John Honey,

February 2, 1748

Bettson, Thomas. Married Jane Merringham,

April 14, 1748

Byram, Millie. Daughter of William and Sarah, born

March 28, 1748

Bridwell, Margaret. Daughter of Jacob, born

January 12, 1748

Balls, John. Son of John and Margaret, born

March 20, 1748

Berry, Benjamin. Son of Richard and Sarah, born

June 10, 1748

Botts, Joseph. Son of Seth, born June 23, 1748

Bush, George. Son of George, born August 10, 1748

Bettson, Thomas. Son of Thomas and Jane, born
July 23, 1748

Berry, Benjamin. Was baptized August 1, 1748

Bussel, Winifred. Married Phillip Payton,
September 15, 1748

Bell, James Wlliam. Son of Andrew and Mary, born
October 14, 1748

Burn, James. Married Catharine Champ,
October 14, 1748

Balls, Ann. Married Samuel Hawes, February 16, 1749

Balls, Edward. Married Sarah Crosby,
November 24, 1749

Berry, Bridget. Married Samuel Mitchel,
January 30, 1749

Basnet, Abrahm. Died February 8, 1749

Bethel, Joseph. Died September 15, 1748

Bethel, Samuel. Son of William, born February 9, 1749

Bethel, Elizabeth. Daughter of Edward and Mary,
born May 26, 1749

Burn, Elizabeth. Was baptized April 16, 1749

Boling, Nancy. Daughter of Edmund and Ann, born
April 26, 1749

Bradley, Nancy. Daughter of David and Margaret,
born April 2, 1749

Bethel, Sith. Married Robert Hammet,
February 7, 1749

Bennet, Nickolas. Married Elizabeth Knight,
June 12, 1749
Barry, Thomas. Married Catharine Jones,
August 5, 1749
Bridwell, John. Son of John and Lucy, born
August 10, 1749
Bridwell, Mealy. Son of Samuel, born August, 1749
Basnett, Ann. Daughter of Isaac and Mary, born
September 3, 1749
Balls, Lydia Beek. Daughter of John and Margaret,
born October 21, 1749
Barbee, Catharine. Was born November 1, 1749
Barbee, Judy. Daughter of Thomas and Margaret,
born October 21, 1749
Bland, Moses. Married Jane Wiggonton,
January 14, 1750
Bridwell, Mealy. Son of Samuel, died
November 8, 1749
Berry, Mary. Daughter of Richard and Sarah, born
January 19, 1749
Baker, John. Son of John, born January 4, 1750
Bromley, Betty. Daughter of William and Judith,
born January 3, 1750
Barbee, Betty. Married William Smith,
January 1, 1750
Bethel, William. Died February 19, 1750

Bridwell, George.   Son of Isaac and Abigal, born
January 26, 1750

Bragg, Peggy.   Daughter of Joseph, born April 9, 1750

Balls, Caleb.   Son of Edward and Sarah, born
April 14, 1750

Boling, Joannah.   Married William Fuell,
February 17, 1750

Byram, Lizzie.   Daughter of William and Sarah,
March 12, 1750

Byram, Cuthbert.   Son of Cuthbert, born
January 6, 1750

Bridwell, Isaac.   Son of Abraham, died May 2, 1750

Bailis, Winifred.   Married Henry Robinson,
August 1, 1750

Bowman, John.   Married Elizabeth Elliot,
December 23, 1750

Bridwell, Margaret.   Married Henry Wiggonton,
November 12, 1750

Bridwell, Betty.   Married Richard Simms,
October 15, 1750

Brent, Catharine.   Wife of George, died
January 21, 1751

Betty, William.   Son of Simpson, born
February 3, 1750

Bell, Jonathan.   Son of George and Ann, born
January 7, 1751

Barby, Ann. Married Garner Burges,

February 19, 1751

Burges, Garner. Married Ann Barby,

February 19, 1751

Barbee, William. Son of Thomas, born April 3, 1751

Botts, Elizabeth. Died April 17, 1751

Bailly, Thomas. Married Ann Waller, July 10, 1751

Burges, Peggy. Daughter of Garner and Ann, born

July 27, 1751

Botts, Joshua. Son of Seth, born July 24, 1751

Balls, Sarah. Wife of Edward, died July 24, 1751

Burn, Judith. Daughter of James, born May 24, 1751

Bayles, Betty. Daughter of John and Mary, born

October 20, 1751

Balls, George. Son of John, Jr., and Margaret, born

October 9, 1751

Bethel, Sith. Daughter of Edward and Mary, born

March 10, 1751

Belsher, Merriam. Married Alexander Manatear,

December 24, 1751

Bush, John. Son of George and Mary, born

December 20, 1751.

Balls, Mollie. Daughter of Henry and Isabel, born

December 13, 1751

Baxter, Alexander. Married Mary Byram,

November 28, 1751

Byram, Mary.   Married Alexander Baxter,
                              November 28, 1751
Bouchard, William.   Married Mary Stringfellow,
                              November 12, 1751
Brown, John.   Married Hannah Cook,
                              November 28, 1751
Bridwell, Benjamin.   Son of John, born April 15, 1752
Bragg, Phœbe.   Daughter of Joseph, born
                              March 25, 1752
Boling, William.   Son of Edmund and Mary, born
                              March 8, 1752
Brooks, Sarah.   Married John Wilson,
                              February 7, 1752
Batto, Lithy.   Daughter of James and Winifred, born
                              February 17, 1752
Bailis, Mary.   Daughter of John and Mary, baptized
                              January 19, 1752
Berry, Sarah.   Daughter of Richard and Sarah, born
                              January 13, 1752
Bannister, Nathan.   Married Ann Eaves, May 24, 1752
Barbee, Thomas.   Son of Thomas, born
                              October 18, 1752
Beach, James.   Died at William Wright's,
                              December 17, 1752
Betty, Ann.   Daughter of Simpson and Elizabeth,
                              born February 9, 1753

Bruing, William. Married Keziah Simmons,
February 4, 1753
Brent, Catharine. Married James Wren,
March 27, 1753
Bradley, Margaret. Wife of David, died
January 3, 1753
Burchel, William. Departed this life at George Hinson's, April 14, 1753
Byron, Sarah. Daughter of William and Sarah, born
May 28, 1753
Brown, Rauleigh Travers. Son of John and Hannah,
born July 13, 1753
Benson, Catharine. Daughter of Charles and Judith,
born August 29, 1753
Bell, George. Son of George and Ann, born
August 12, 1753
Burn, Catharine. Daughter of James and Catharine,
born August 3, 1753
Balls, Hezhzeba. Son of John, baptized
July 1, 1753
Beach, George. Married Susanna Duke,
December 23, 1753
Bridwell, Elizabeth. Daughter of Jacob and Elizabeth,
born December 26, 1753
Bridwell, Isaac. Son of Isaac and Abigal, born
December 9, 1753

Byram, Winifred.   Married William Routt,
                                November 27, 1753
Burton, William.   Married Rachel Porch,
                                October 7, 1753
Brent, Mary.   Married William Wright,
                                October 18, 1753
Bell, George.   Son of George and Ann, baptized
                                October 1, 1753
Bridwell, Samuel.   Drowned in Quantico Run,
                                November 27, 1753
Burges, Mollie.   Daughter of Garner, baptized
                                December 9, 1753
Berry, William.   Son of Richard and Sarah, born
                                January 12, 1754
Bussel, George.   Married Catharine Randel,
                                January 8, 1754
Bailis, Jesse.   Son of John and Mary, born
                                February 4, 1754
Berry, William.   Married Ann Porch,
                                February, 26, 1754
Bussel, James.   Married Martha Hill,
                                February 24, 1754
Bethel, Edward.   Son of Edward, born
                                April 30, 1754
Battoo, John Holliday.   Son of James, baptized
                                May 19, 1754

Beach, Susannah. Daughter of George and Susannah,
                              baptized August 18, 1754
Bell, John. Son of Thomas and Mary, born
                              July 26, 1754
Brown, Joshua. Married Alice Lunsford,
                              July 21, 1754
Brent, James. Son of Charles, died
                              September 6, 1754
Brent, Catharine. Married James Douglass,
                              October 1, 1754
Bridwell, George. Son of John and Lucy, born
                              December 10, 1754
Bussel, Thomas. Son of James and Martha, born
                              November 15, 1754
Barbee, John. Son of Thomas, was born
                              November 12, 1754
Balls, William. Son of Henry and Isabel, born
                              December 14, 1754
Botts, John. Son of Sith and Lib, born
                              October 25, 1754
Balls, Nathanel William. Son of John, Jr., baptized
                              January 26, 1754
Bridwell, George. Son of John and Lucy, baptized
                              January 26, 1755
Burges, William. Married Bathsueba Courtney,
                              January 19, 1755

Bradley, David.   Married Elizabeth Simmons,
                                    April 17, 1755
Brown, John.   Married Jean Noland, August 24, 1755
Burk, John.   Married Elizabeth Farlow,
                                    August 31, 1755
Bethany, Thomas.   Married Mary Ann Criswell,
                                    December 21, 1755
Bell, George.   Son of George and Ann, born
                                    September 3, 1755
Bell, Elizabeth.   Was baptized September 28, 1755
Bussell, Agathy.   Daughter of William, baptized
                                    October 26, 1755
Byram, Nancy.   Daughter of John, baptized
                                    November 2, 1755
Burton, Samuel.   Son of William and Rachel, born
                                    April 20, 1756
Betty, Lottie.   Daughter of Simpson and Elizabeth,
                                    born April 11, 1756
Bridwell, Samuel.   Son of Jacob and Elizabeth, born
                                    March 6, 1756
Botts, Sarah.   Married James Wiggonton,
                                    February 9, 1756
Benson, Enoch.   Married Mary Doial,
                                    February 15, 1756
Barby, Sarah.   Daughter of Thomas and Margaret,
                                    born January 28, 1756

Brown, Cicy.   Was baptized January 18, 1756

Brent, Charles.   Departed this life January 13, 1756

Brent, Mary.   Married Zackrias Lewis,
>
> August 24, 1756

Bethel, Mary.   Daughter of Edward, born
>
> August 10, 1756

Bell, Thomas.   Son of Thomas, born
>
> December 24, 1756

Bolling, Elizabeth.   Married Robert Mays,
>
> December 27, 1756

Balls, Heptizitah.   Son of John, Jr., died
>
> December 17, 1756

Blueford, Jemimma.   Married Robert English,
>
> November 22, 1756

Brown, William.   Married Sarah Ellen Grogg,
>
> December 11, 1756

Brent, Susanna.   Married Dr. John Southland,
>
> September 15, 1756

Baylis, Christopher.   Son of Jean, born
>
> September 9, 1756

Bell, William.   Son of James, was born
>
> January 11, 1757

Baylis, William.   Married Ann Gough,
>
> January 19, 1757

Brooke, Hannah.   Married Alexander Taylor,
>
> February 24, 1757

Brent, Jane.   Married Richard Graham,

February 10, 1757

Bussell, Anna.   Daughter of James and Martha, born

April 11, 1757

Barbee, Betty.   Daughter of Thomas, born

March 23, 1757

Brown, Pearson.   Was baptized March 6, 1757

Bridwell, Simon.   Son of John and Lucy, born

August 11, 1757

Botts, Jenny.   Daughter of Seth and Lib, born

January 8, 1757

Bussel, Betty.   Daughter of Hannah, born

February 7, 1756

Blackburn, Edward.   Married Margaret Harrison

May 26, 1757

Bruing, Ann.   Married Saxfield Noxal,

August 8, 1757

Boling, Elizabeth.   Daughter of Edmund and Mary,

born October 30, 1757

Butcher, James.   Son of William and Mary, born

September 10, 1757

Balls, Charles.   Son of John and Margaret, born

February 13, 1758

Bussel, ———.   Married Sarah Day, February 5, 1758

Byram, Peter.   Married Martha Horton,

March 26, 1758

Bradley, William.   Married Margaret Fortick,

March 28, 1758

Bridwell, ————.   Married Lucy Lea, April 9, 1758

Barbee, Joseph.   Son of Thomas and Margaret,

baptized June 28, 1758

Bush, Elizabeth.   Daughter of George and Mary,

born February 20, 1758

C

Carter, John.   Son of James and Mary, born

May 7, 1727

Carter, James.   Son of James and Mary, born

March 31, 1729

Carter, William.   Son of James and Mary, born

January 11, 1731

Carter, George.   Son of James and Mary, born

March 25, 1733

Carter, Catharine.   Daughter of James and Mary,

born April 1, 1735

Carpenter, Stephen.   Son of John and Mary, born

June 24, 1737

Crosby, Uriel.   Son of George and Sarah, born

August 19, 1738

Courtney, Anne.   Married Henry Foley,

December 24, 1738

Cornish, Charles.   Married Elizabeth Smith,

December 17, 1738

Chapman, Jane. Daughter of Taylor and Margaret,
born January 25, 1739

Chimp, William. Married Catharine Taylor,
January 31, 1739

Colson, Charles. Married Elizabeth Norton.
February 1, 1739

Carpenter, John. Son of John and Mary, born
May 15, 1739

Chapman, Taylor. Married Margaret Markham,
September 13, 1739

Chapman, Jane. Daughter of Taylor and Margaret,
born January 25, 1741

Chambers, Sarah. Married William McDuell,
December 26, 1739

Cosby, James. Son of Peter and Susannah, born
February 27, 1740

Cooper, Joseph. Son of Joseph and Elizabeth, born
July 22, 1740

Chin, Lettie. Daughter of Rawleigh and Elizabeth,
born October 17, 1740

Clutterbuck, Mary. Daughter of William and Mary,
born October 25, 1740

Carter, Hugh. Son of James and Mary,
born November 8, 1740

Combs, William. Son of Mason and Sarah, born
November 28, 1740

Carberry, James. Son of Edward and Mary, born
November 17, 1740

Chapman, Jane. Daughter of Taylor, died
December 12, 1740

Carberry, Edward. Departed this life
February 24, 1741

Clark, Catherine. Died at James Suddith's, May 7, 1741

Cave, James. Son of William and Anne, born
April 24, 1741

Combs, Jean. Married John Ashby, May 11, 1741

Campbell, James. Married Elizabeth Milliner,
September 27, 1741

Crosby, Ann. Daughter of George and Sarah, born
October 1, 1741

Chapman, William. Son of Taylor and Margaret,
born September 12, 1741

Carney, Thomas. Son of John and Mary, born
December 18, 1741

Cockley, Robert. Married Sarah Sinclair,
September 21, 1740

Coffy, Frances. Daughter of Peter, died
January 5, 1741

Coffee, James. Son of Peter and Susannah, born
February 27, 1741

Coffee, Lydia. Daughter of Peter and Susannah, born
January 25, 1742

Cook, Jane.   Married William Pritchet,
                              January 26, 1742
Cassity, Catherine.   Married Philip Mathews,
                              January 4, 1742
Cooper, Juhonias.   Son of Joseph and Betty, born
                              February 20, 1742
Cammel, William.   Married Mary Smith,
                              July 25, 1742
Cave, William.   Died at his house, August 14, 1742
Cole, Catharine.   Married Philip Prichet,
                              June 24, 1742
Craven, Francesana.   Married Samuel Makanes,
                              November 14, 1742
Cave, James.   Son of William and Anne, died
                              January 6, 1743
Cotton, John.   Married Susannah Smith,
                              February 17, 1743
Combs, Anne.   Daughter of Mason and Sarah, born
                              March 28, 1743
Champ, John.   Son of William and Catharine, born
                              March 10, 1743
Corbin, William.   Married Sarah Jenkins,
                              January 1, 1743
Champ, John.   Son of William, died August 6, 1743
Carter, Charles.   Son of James, born
                              October 10, 1743

Carter, James.   An honest, good man, died .

October 24, 1743

Coffee, Benjamin.   Son of Peter and Susannah, born

October 9, 1743

Cooper, John.   Son of Joseph and Elizabeth, born

December 4, 1743

Carney, Traverse.   Son of John and Mary, born

January 17, 1744

Carney, Daniel.   Son of John and Mary, died

January 28, 1744

Crosby, George.   Married Mary Huges,

January 6, 1744

Crosby, Sally.   Daughter of George and Sarah, born

March 3, 1744

Cunningham, William.   Son of Morris, born

March 21, 1744

Carpenter, Thomas.   Son of John and Mary, born

August 7, 1744

Carter, Dale.   Son of Charles and Lucy, born

August 9, 1744

Corbin, William.   Married Sarah Want,

August 2, 1744

Champ, Lansdell.   Daughter of William and

Catharine, born December 1, 1744

Coffey, Mary.   Married James Kendal,

February 25, 1745

Carney, Absolom. Son of John and Mary, born
January 27, 1745
Combs, Sarah. Daughter of Mason and Sarah, born
February 25, 1745
Cotney, William. Married Mary Barbee,
February 24, 1745
Cooper, Enos. Son of Joseph and Elizabeth, born
April 26, 1745
Carter, John. Married Mary Butler,
February 4, 1745
Carpenter, William. Son of John and Mary, born
May 5, 1742
Clarnes, Ann. Married Andrew Kenney,
November 30, 1744
Carter, Ann. Married Joseph Butler,
November 28, 1745
Cooper, John. Married Elizabeth Pownall,
March 30, 1745
Cannon, John. Married Sarah Broderick,
July 8, 1745
Carr, Easter. Married Peter Reynolds, June 2, 1745
Crosby, Anne. Daughter of George and Mary, born
May 30, 1745
Crosby, George. Departed this life, December 5, 1745
Chinn, Lizzie. Daughter of Betty, born
October 18, 1745

Cooke, Elizabeth. Departed this life,

> October 20, 1745

Cavenaugh, Edward. Died at Rawleigh Chinn's,

> January 11, 1742

Crosby, Anne. Daughter of George, died

> October 31, 1745

Crosby, Sally. Daughter of George and Mary, died

> October 28, 1745

Cotney, John. Son of William, born

> November 10, 1745

Corbin, Peter. Son of William and Sarah, born

> April 23, 1745

Camp, Hannah. Daughter of Mary, born

> March 26, 1746

Cash, Peter. Son of Peter and Charity, born

> July 17, 1746

Carter, Joseph. Married Margaret Mason,

> November 27, 1746

Champe, Rosomond. Daughter of William and

> Catharine, born November 18, 1746

Castello, Ann. Married Richard Sayer,

> September 30, 1746

Carpenter, Benjamin. Son of John and Mary, born

> October 5, 1746

Combs, Mason. Son of Mason and Sarah, born

> February 21, 1747

Carter, Judith.   Daughter of Charles and Lucy, born
March 17, 1747
Cannaday, William.   Married Margaret Linee,
January, 16, 1747
Crosby, George.   Son of George and Mary, born
September 1, 1747
Carney, Mary.   Daughter of John and Mary, born
October 16, 1747
Cave, Elizabeth.   Married Keene Withers,
December 21, 1747
Cave, Ann.   Married Thomas Dent,
December 3, 1747
Connally, Dorothy.   Married Robert Read,
November 10, 1747
Champ, William.   Departed this life,
November 13, 1747
Carter, Mary Ann.   Daughter of Joseph and Margaret,
born December 7, 1747
Corbin, John.   Son of William and Sarah, born
November 22, 1747
Cannon, Ellis.   Son of John and Sarah, born
January 3, 1748
Courtney, Elizabeth.   Daughter of William, born
January 1, 1748
Carter, Robert.   Son of Robert and Winifred, born
February 14, 1748

Chinn, Betty. Married Solomon Waugh,

April 13, 1748

Cooper, Thomas Simmons. Son of Joseph, born

May 29, 1748

Chinn, Rawleigh. Married Sarah Lacy,

September 2, 1748

Carpenter, Ann. Daughter of John and Mary, born

October 16, 1748

Champ, Catharine. Married to James Burns,

October 14, 1748

Clarke, Lucy. Married Stephen Pilcher,

December 7, 1748

Crosby, Sarah. Married Edward Balls,

November 24, 1748

Carpenter, Nanny. Daughter of John, baptized

November 27, 1748

Carty, Peter Murphy. Son of Honour, died

December 1, 1748

Cowper, Thomas Simmons. Son of Joseph, died

February 2, 1749

Crump, Benjamin. Married Hannah James,

February 2, 1749

Corbin, Mary. Daughter of William and Sarah,

baptized April 9, 1749

Chinn, Margaret. Daughter of Rawleigh and Sarah,

born May 14, 1749

Combs, Winny.   Daughter of Mason and Sarah, born
May 14, 1749

Congers, Sarah Pattison.   Married Thomas Hampton,
June 1, 1749

Cash, Elizabeth.   Married Calvert Porter,
September 21, 1749

Cooper, Spencer.   Son of Joseph, born
October 22, 1749

Corbin, John.   Married Frances Fant,
December 7, 1749

Cooke, Margaret.   Married William Horton,
December 21, 1749

Carney, Jane.   Daughter of John and Mary, born
December 21, 1749

Corbin, William.   Was born November 10, 1749

Cartee, Honour.   Delivered of a male child, which
died soon after, November 20, 1749

Chapman, Taylor.   Departed this life
November 10, 1749

Cannon, John.   Son of John, born February 1, 1749

Conyers, Ann Holland.   Married Edward Payne,
February 27, 1750

Carter, Lucy.   Daughter of Charles and Lucy, born
February 16, 1750

Cornell, John.   Son of Margaret, born March 31, 1750

Crap, James.   Married Joyie Hinson, June 3, 1750

Cooper, Bridget. Married John Sylva, July 1, 1750
Cabbage, John.   Married May Jenkins,
                                    July 10, 1750
Carter, Mary.   Daughter of Robert and Winifred,
                                    born May 21, 1750
Cash, Elizabeth. Was baptized June 24, 1750
Chinn, Hannah.   Married John Risen,
                                    October 20, 1750
Carty, Honora.   Married John Adams,
                                    September 23, 1750
Carter, Judith. Daughter of Charles and Lucy, died
                                    December 18, 1750
Corbin, William. Son of John and Francis, born
                                    February 7, 1751
Collie, James.   Married Ann Cornwall,
                                    February 21, 1751
Cornwall, Ann.   Married James Collie,
                                    February 21, 1751
Cash, Elizabeth. Departed this life, March 9, 1751
Cash, Jean.   Married William Waters, April 6, 1751
Chinn, ———.   Married Mathew Gregg,
                                    August 15, 1751
Carter, Lucy.   Daughter of Charles and Lucy, died
                                    August 22, 1751
Cartee, Thomas. Died at Stephen Pilcher's,
                                    June 18, 1751

Carter, Solomon.   Married Mary Marony,

> May 26, 1751

Cannaday, Franky.   Daughter of John and Rose, born

> May 29, 1751

Cabbige, Elizabeth.   Daughter of John and Mary,

> born April 7, 1751

Cook, Hannah.   Married John Brown,

> November 28, 1751

Cooper, Vinient.   Son of Joseph and Elizabeth, born

> October 10, 1751

Combs, Wilmot.   Daughter of Mason, born

> October 5, 1751

Corbin, Margaret.   Daughter of William and Sarah,

> born January 17, 1752

Cannon, Henry.   Son of John and Sarah, born

> April 10, 1752

Cooper, Vinient.   Son of Joseph and Elizabeth, died

> March 15, 1752

Condring, Jane.   Daughter of Richard, born

> January 11, 1752

Conwell, Barnet.   Son of Margaret, born

> April 17, 1752

Carter, James.   Son of John, Jr., baptized

> August 30, 1752

Carter, Jedisiah.   Son of Robert, was born

> July 29, 1752

Carter, James. Son of John and Leana, born
                                July 17, 1752
Cocklen, Margaret. Married William Todd,
                                October 23, 1752
Carney, Sarah. Married John Anderson,
                                November 28, 1752
Carter, Margaret. Wife of Joseph, died
                                March 12, 1752
Carter, Margaret. Daughter of Joseph, born
                                March 11, 1752
Cooper, Jess. Son of Joseph and Elizabeth, born
                                April 14, 1753
Cubbige, Mary. Daughter of John, born
                                April 15, 1753
Carpenter, George. Son of John and Mary, born
                                March 24, 1753
Cannaday, Sethe. Married Edward Gill,
                                February 4, 1753
Cannaday, Ann. Daughter of John and Rosanna,
                                born March 2, 1753
Carter, Catharine. Daughter of Jeremiah, born
                                January 28, 1753
Carter, Elizabeth. Daughter of Solomon, baptized
                                January 15, 1753
Coleman, John. Son of John and Isabel, born
                                August 6, 1753

Chinn, Ann.   Daughter of Rawleigh, Jr., born
December 15, 1754

Crap, John.   Son of James, Jr., was born
October 7, 1753

Carter, Catharine.   Daughter of Charles, born
October 15, 1753

Cash, James.   Son of Peter and Charity, born
October 26, 1753

Colburn, John.   Son of John, died February 3, 1754

Carter, William.   Died at Mary Edward's,
September 3, 1753

Chinn, Joseph.   Departed this life, January 28, 1754

Cooke, Travers.   Married Mary Doniphan,
February 26, 1754

Carter, Catharine.   Daughter of James, born
April 21, 1754

Carter, John.   Son of John and Leanna, born
June 1, 1754

Carrow, Frances.   Daughter of Mary, born at Richard
Fistoe's, June 29, 1754

Cannon, William.   Son of John and Sarah, born
July 4, 1754

Cuiberford, James.   Married Elizabeth Holdbroke,
September 15, 1754

Carter, Margaret.   Daughter of Joseph, died
October 11, 1754

Cooke, John. Died at Robert Fristoe's,

September 27, 1755

Carney, Oxesby. Son of John and Mary, born

January 2, 1755

Courtney, Bathsheba. Married William Burges,

January 19, 1755

Cooke, John. Son of Travers and Mary, born

February 5, 1755

Carter, Joseph. Married Lettie Linton,

February 5, 1755

Coleman, Lizzie Ann. Daughter of John and Isabel,

born February 12, 1755

Carter, Milly. Daughter of Robert, born

March 22, 1755

Croscuel, Ruth. Married Peter Stacey,

May 25, 1755

Cooke, Ann. Married Thomas Roach,

December 28, 1755

Carter, Anthony. Son of Joseph, born

December 14, 1755

Carter, William. Son of John and Leanna, born

November 22, 1755

Carter, Catharine. Married William Davis,

November 27, 1755

Congers, Theodosia. Married James O'Daneal,

October 19, 1755

Cubbige, William,   Son of John and Mary, born
                                September 29, 1755
Carter, Henry.   Son of Jeremiah, born
                                September 1, 1755
Criswell, Mary Ann.   Married Thomas Bethany,
                                December 21, 1755
Collie, Charles.   Son of James and Ann, born
                                January 25, 1756
Carpenter, Charles.   Son of John and Mary, born
                                September 6, 1756
Cooper, Thomas.   Son of Joseph and Elizabeth, born
                                September 20, 1756
Corbin, James.   Son of John and Frances, born
                                November 8, 1756
Corney, Anthony.   Son of Ann and John, born
                                October 13, 1756
Corney, Henry.   Son of John, baptized
                                November 25, 1756
Cummings, John.   Married Lettice Phillips,
                                February 21, 1757
Cooke, Mott.   Son of Travers and Mary, born
                                March 17, 1757
Cannon, Sarah.   Daughter of John, born
                                June 9, 1757
Carter, Tabitha.   Daughter of Jeremiah, born
                                December 11, 1757

Crosby, Mary. Daughter of George and Mary, born
November 14, 1757
Coleman, Jesse. Son of John and Isabel, born
September 3, 1757
Cooper, William. Married Elizabeth Pliford,
January 5, 1758
Carter, Andrew. Son of Joseph, born June 16, 1758

D.

Daniel, Peter. Married Sarah Travers, July 15, 1736
Daniel, Hannah. Daughter of Peter and Sarah, born
September 9, 1737
Dillon, Anne. Married William Hacker, May 21, 1738
Davison, Andrew. Married Sarah McInteer,
November 5, 1738
Dows, Annie. Married William Miller,
March 5, 1738
Davison, James. Son of Andrew and Sarah, born
November 22, 1739
Dunaway, Mary. Daughter of Samuel and Elizabeth,
born January 6, 1740
Dunaway, Mary. Married James Stuart,
February 12, 1740
Doniphon, Alexander. Married Mary Waugh,
June 17, 1740
Dawist, Samuel. Son of Arthur, died
September 1, 1740

Duffy, Stela. Daughter of Margaret, born
November 28, and died December 4, 1740
Daniel, Travers. Son of Travers and Francis, born
August 4, and baptized privately,
August 5, 1768
Daniel, Travers. Son of Peter and Sarah, born
May 26, 1741
Daniel, Travers, and Frances Moncure, Jr., were mar-
ried at "Claremont" October 7, 1762, by
the Rev. Mr. James Scott.
Dalton, James. Son of James and Rachel, born
July 10, 1741
Davison, Andrew. Son of Andrew and Sarah, born
January 9, 1742
Dunaway, Sarah. Married James Marten,
January 22, 1741
Dent, Arthur. Married Elizabeth Manuel,
December 11, 1742
Doniphan, William. Son of Alexander and Mary,
born March 20, 1742
Duwest, Elizabeth. Married Morton Holiday,
July 28, 1742
Day, Francis. Son of Francis and Mary, born
September 29, 1742
Dillon, James. Married Margaret Warner,
.November 16, 1742

Doniphon, Anne. Married George White,

August 4, 1743

Dent, Mary. Daughter of Arthur and Elizabeth,

born November 8, 1743

Dunaway, Laton. Son of Daniel, died

January 31, 1744

Dunaway, Daniel. Married Jean Judd,

March 1, 1744

Doniphon, Elizabeth. Daughter of Alexander and

Mary, born April 18, 1744

Dawson, Jean. Married George Knight,

December 25, 1744

Dobie, Anne. Daughter of Anne, born

October 25, 1744

Davison, William. Son of Andrew and Sarah, born

October 25, 1745

Day, John. Son of Francis and Mary, born

February 8, 1745

Dickinson, Mary. Daughter of Ann and Edward

born February 15, 1745

Dunaway, Charity. Daughter of Joseph, born

March 7, 1745

Dunaway, Gothe. Daughter of Joseph and Elizabeth,

born May 22, ——

Daniel, Elizabeth Travers. Daughter of Peter and

Sarah, born May 16, 1745

Dalton, Anne.   Daughter of John, baptized
September 29, 1745

Dent, Anne.   Married William Black,
October 17, 1745

Duncomb, Rosamond.   Married Anthony Horten,
October 27, 1745

Dent, James.   Son of Arthur, born
December 21, 1745

Dinwiddie, Elizabeth.   Married Gerrard Fowke,
November 26, 1745

Davids, Elizabeth.   Daughter of John and Ann, born
March 2, 1745

Deckon, Margaret.   Married James Reynold,
August 19, 1746

Dillon, James.   Married Ann Suddeth,
July 24, 1746

Doniphon, Anne.   Daughter of Alexander and Mary,
born February 28, 1747

Davis, Thomas.   Son of John, born August 8, 1747

Day, Mary Ann.   Daughter of Frances, born
September 28, 1747

Dent, Thomas.   Married Ann Cave, December 3, 1747

Donaldson, John.   Married Ann McMurry,
December 31, 1747

Dunaway, Jean.   Daughter of Joseph, born
January 2, 1748

Devane, Mary. Married John Herrod,

August 21, 1748

Davis, John. Son of John, was born

November 11, 1748

Dunaway, Eton. Son of Daniel, born April 12, 1749

Dunaway, Eton. Son of Daniel, died

September 9, 1749

Dunawoy, Ezekiel. Was baptized July 23, 1749

Dawson, Christopher. Married Jane George,

February 16, 1750

Doniphan, Alexander. Son of Alexander and Mary,

born March 12, 1750

Davis, Nanny. Daughter of John, born

March 28, 1750

Dunaway, Jane. Wife of Daniel, died

October 28, 1750

Dunaway, Isaac. Son of Daniel, born

September 20, 1750

Dooling, Nancy. Daughter of Robert, born

October 31, 1750

Day, Margaret. Daughter of Francis, born

January 2, 1751

Daffin, Keziah. Daughter of Judith and Henry, born

March 30, 1751

Dooling, Margaret. Daughter of John, born

December 25, 1751

Dunaway, Daniel. Departed this life,
                              December 12, 1751
Dunaway, Elizabeth. Married Benjamin Lokon,
                              February 25, 1752
Doyson, John. Son of Christopher and Jean, boan
                              July 28, 1751
Dooling, Mary Ann. Daughter of Robert, born
                              April 5, 1753
Donophon, Mott. Son of Alexander and Mary, born
                              June 10, 1752
Davis, Susannah. Married Richard Smith,
                              November 17, 1752
Dial, Mitchel. Married Mary Smith,
                              November 19, 1752
Davis, Isaac. Son of John, born February 7, 1753
Dick, Moses. Son of Jane, born January 23, 1753
Duwest, Elizabeth. Daughter of Mary, born
                              January 6, 1753
Duke, Susanna. Married George Beach,
                              December 23, 1753
Dawson, Sarah. Daughter of Jean and Christopher,
                              born September 15, 1753
Doniphon, Mary. Married Travers Cooke,
                              February 26, 1754
Dowling, Nicholas. Married Elizabeth Dunaway,
                              June 30, 1754

Dunaway, Elizabeth. Married Nicholas Dowling,
June 30, 1754

Dunaway, Isaac. Married Mary Ann Tolson,
May 25, 1754

Dawson, Henry. Married Betty Turner,
December 15, 1754

Dooling, James. Son of Robert, born May 9, 1755

Douglass, James. Married Catharine Brent,
October 1, 1754

Dabney, George. Married Mary Waller,
September 11, 1754

Dawson, William and Henry. Sons of Jean and
Christopher, born May 27, 1755

Diskin, John. Married Frances MacCarty,
June 19, 1755

Dawson, Sarah. Daughter of Christopher, died
July 15, 1755

Dawson, William and Henry. Died June 15, 1755

Davis, William. Married Catharine Carter,
November 27, 1755

Duwest, Elizabeth. Married George Mason,
October 21, 1755

Doial, Mary. Married Enoch Benson,
February 15, 1756

Dawson, Henry. Son of Christopher, born
June 27, 1756

Driscol, Derby.   Married Jean Noble, October 4, 1756

Douglass, George.   Son of James and Catharine, born
December 2, 1756

Dooling, Nancy.   Daughter of Nicholas, died
October 24, 1756

Douglass, George.   Departed this life,
December 17, 1756

Daniel, Hannah.   Married George Hedgman,
November 27, 1756

Day, Robert.   Married Mary Gunn, January 16, 1757

Day, Winny.   Daughter of Roberson and Mary, born
October 15, 1758

Dunaway, Benjamin.   Son of Isaac and Mary, born
November, 27, 1757

Day, Sarah.   Married ——— Bussel, February 5, 1758

Darlow, Thomas.   Married Margaret Lynne,
April 9, 1758

Dawson, Jane.   Daughter of Christopher and Jane,
born March 14, 1758

E.

Edwards, Elizabeth.   Married William King,
May 21, 1738

Eaves, William.   Son of Thomas and Catharine, born
November 9, 1739

Elkin, David.   Son of William and Martha, born
February 14, 1742

Edwards, Jess.   Son of Ignatius and Mary, born
                                    February 14, 1742
Elliot, Samuel.   Married Easter Flood, August 9, 1742
Eaves, Thomas.   Son of Thomas and Catharine, born
                                    August 15, 1742
Eaves, Anne.   The wife of Thomas, died
                                    February 6, 1742
Edrington, Thomas.   Son of Wllliam, born
                                    August 17, 1743
Edwards, John.   Son of Ignatius, died
                                    February 24, 1744
Edwards, James.   Son of Meredith and Mary, born
                                    February 22, 1744
Eaton, Mary.   Daughter of William, born
                                    May 22, 1744
Ellis, Sith.   Daughter of John and Sarah, born
                                    July 22, 1745
Edwards, Ignatius.   Had a daughter Anne, by Mary,
                                    July 17, 1745
Edwards, James.   Departed this life October 11, 1745
Edwards, Elizabeth.   Daughter of Meredith and Mary,
                                    born December 22, 1746
Eaves, Winifred.   Married Peter Wigginton,
                                    October 13, 1747
Elliot, Samuel.   Married Elizabeth Wiggerson,
                                    May 20, 1747

Eaton, Sarah.   Daughter of William, baptized
                        September 20, 1747
Edwards, John.   Son of Robert and Sarah, born
                        March 20, 1748
Edwards, Meredith.   Son of Meredith and Mary, born
                        September 12, 1749
Edwards, Sarah.   Daughter of Ignatius and Mary,
                        born June 28, 1748
Elkins, Margaret.   Daughter of William, born
                        August 7, 1747
Elliot, Ann.   Daughter of Samuel and Elizabeth, born
                        July 10, 1748
Elliot, Samuel.   Departed this life, November 30, 1748
Edrington, Christopher.   Son of William, born
                        April 16, 1749
Edwards, Meredith.   Departed this life
                        October 16, 1749
Edwards, Matthews.   Son of Robert and Sarah, born
                        August 27, 1749
Ellis, Millis.   Was baptized September 30, 1750
Edwards, Ignatius.   Departed this life,
                        October 15, 1750
Elliot, Elizabeth.   Married John Bowman,
                        December 23, 1750
Edrington, Ann.   Daughter of William, born
                        March 19, 1751

Edwards, Andrew. Married Betty Waugh,

May 7, 1751

Eaves, Thomas. Departed this life March 10, 1752

Edwards, Betty. Daughter of Andrew and Betty,

born February 7, 1752

Edwards, Betty. Daughter of Andrew and Be tty,

died August 23, 1753

Edwards, Billy. Son of Andrew and Betty, born

October 1, 1753

Eaves, Ann. Married Nathan Bannister,

˙May 24, 1752

Edrington, John. Son of William, born

November 14, 1753

Ellis, Jezreel. Son of Sarah, born August 28, 1753

Edghill, Jean. Daughter of Thomas, born

March 18, 1754

Edwards, Jean. Daughter of Robert and Sarah, born

September 29, 1754

Edzar, James. Married Eleanor Grianan,

November 22, 1754

Earle, Therdosian Scott. Daughter of Samuel and

Elizabeth, born November 14, 1754

Edwards, Bridget. Married Jeremiah Spilman,

January 16, 1758

Edgar, Esdras. Son of James and Eleanor, born

February 25, 1758

Edwards, William.   Married Eleanor Wheeler,
                              February 12, 1756
Edrington, James.   Son of William and Betty, born
                              February 24, 1756
Edwards, Robert.   Son of Robert and Sarah, born
                              February 6, 1756
Edwards, Nancy.   Daughter of Andrew and Betty,
                              born March 6, 1756
Eaves, Hannah.   ·Married John Stark, May 29, 1756
English, Rose.   Daughter of John and Mary, born
                              May 30, 1756
Earle, Betty.   Daughter of Samuel and Elizabeth,
                              born September 6, 1756
English, Robert.   Married Jemima Blueford,
                              November 22, 1756
English, Sarah.   Daughter of Robert and Jemima,
                              born January 23, 1757
Edwards, Isaker.   Married Sarah Stacey, May 16, 1757
Edwards, Andrew.   Married Elizabeth Withers,
                              January 19, 1758

F.

Fowke, William Chandler.   Son of Chandler and
                              Mary, born September 4, 1720
Fowke, John.   Son of Chandler and Mary, born
                              January 17, 1725

Fowke, Elizabeth. Daughter of Chandler and Mary,
born April 27, 1727
Fowke, Chandler. The young son of Chandler and
Mary, born September 3, 1732
Fowke, Ann. Younger daughter of Chandler and
Mary, born September 4, 1737
Fowke, Sarah. Daughter of Chandler and Mary, born
August 10, 1734
Fowke, Ann. Daughter of Chandler and Mary, died
December 8, 1732
Fowke, Sarah. Daughter of Chandler and Mary, died
October 14, 1739
Fowke, Susannah. Daughter of Chandler and Mary,
born October 24, 1739
Frogg, John. Married Elizabeth Strother,
November 9, 1738
Foley, Henry. Married Anne Courtney,
December 24, 1738
Fristoe, Daniel. Son of Richard, Jr. and Grace, born
December 7, 1739
Fowke, John. Son of Chandler and Mary, died
April 16, 1740
French, Betty. Married James Waugh,
August 22, 1740
Fristoe, John. Son of Richard and Grace, born
June 6, 1741

Fowke, Richard.   Son of Chandler and Mary, born
December 11, 1741

Foley, Hannah.   Daughter of John and Rosina, born
April 20, 1742

Fristoe, William.   Son of Richard, died
May 12, 1742

Fristoe, Richard.   Son of Richard and Grace, born
July 9, 1742

Flood, Easter.   Married Samuel Elliot,
August 9, 1742

Fowke, William.   Departed this life,
October 24, 1742

Fletcher, George.   Married Sarah Grigsby,
January 1, 1743

Fowke, William.   Son of Chandler and Mary, born
May 31, 1743

Fletcher, Sarah.   Daughter of Charles, born
May 31, 1743

Foley, Mary.   Married Benjamin Stringfellow,
June 15, 1743

Fant, Catharine.   Married Alexander Simpson,
July 17, 1743

Fowke, William.   Son of Chandler and Mary, died
December 2, 1743

Fristoe, George.   Son of Richard and Grace, born
April 10, 1744

Foley, John. Married Sarah Poole,

December 11, 1744

Fling, John. Married Mary Briand,

December 31, 1744

French, Margaret. Married Peter Hansbrough,

February 26, 1745

Fowke, Captain Chandler, of Gunston Hall, in Stafford

County. Died February 10, 1745

Fant, George. Son of William and Catharine, born

June 5, 1745

Fristoe, Jean. Daughter of Richard and Grace, born

September 8, 1745

Fowke, Gerrard. Married Elizabeth Dinwiddie,

November 26, 1745

Fletcher, Sarah. Daughter of Charles, baptized

May 31, 1746

Fletcher, Elizabeth. Married Benjamin Allenthrop,

August 19, 1746

Foster, George. Married Margaret Grigsby,

December 22, 1746

Fletcher, Abraham. Married Priscilla Grigsby,

November 28, 1746

Fowke, Robert Dinwiddie. Son of Gerrard and

Elizabeth, born September 20, 1746

Fristoe, William. Son of Richard and Grace, born

March 29, 1747

Fitzhugh, Catharine.   The wife of Thomas, died
February 26, 1748
Fristoe, George.   Son of Richard, died May 12, 1748
Fant, Margaret.   Married Thomas Barbee,
September 29, 1748
Fristoe, Richard.   Married Mary Hayes,
November 24, 1748
Fernsly, James.   Married Sarah Robinson,
December 3, 1748
Foregast, James.   Died at William Wright's,
December 15, 1748
Fristoe, George.   Son of Richard and Grace, born
January 8, 1749
Fant, Nathaniel.   Son of William and Catharine, born
January 15, 1749
Foley, Barrett.   Son of John and Rosanna, born
February 14, 1749
Ford, Mary.   Daughter of David and Mary, born
February 9, 1749
Fletcher, George.   Departed this life March 16, 1749
Foster William.   Married Nanny Jordan,
June 15, 1749
Fant, Frances.   Married John Corbin,
December 7, 1740
Fuell, William.   Married Johannah Boling,
February 12, 1750

Fristoe, George.   Son of Richard and Grace, died
December 7, 1750

Foxworthy, Sarah.   Married Daniel Green,
October 16, 1750

Fuell, Eleanor.   Daughter of William and Hannah,
born October 9, 1750

Foster, Elizabeth.   Daughter of William and Ann,
born February 26, 1751

Ford, David.   Son of David, born April 1, 1751

Fristoe, Robert.   Son of Richard and Grace, born
April 5, 1751

Fristoe, Mary.   Departed this life March 26, 1751

Fristoe, Martha.   Married Josuah King,
December 12, 1751

Foxworthy, Thomas.   Married Sarah Nubal,
December 25, 1751

Fritter, Moses.   Married Elizabeth Horton,
December 1, 1751

Foxworthy, John.   Married Sarah Northcut,
September 29, 1751

Fitzpatrick, Thomas.   Son of John and Mary, born
February 26, 1752

Foxworthy, Nickolas.   Married Mary Jordon,
January 26, 1752

Fristoe, Robert.   Married Ann Rhodes,
February 23, 1752

Fitzpatrick, John.   Married Mary Waters,
                                February 12, 1752
Floyd, Betty Ann.   Daughter of James, born
                                June 1, 1752
Fritter, John.   Son of Moses and Elizabeth, born
                                December 18, 1752
Foxworthy, John.   Son of Mary and Thomas, born
                                February 2, 1753
Fernsby, Sarah.   Daughter of James and Sarah,
                                born February 10, 1753
Foster, Isabelle.   Daughter of William and Ann, born
                                February 16, 1753
Foxworthy, Catharine.   Daughter of Nickolas and
                                Mary, born March 23, 1753
Foxworthy, William.   Son of John and Sarah, born
                                April 1, 1753
Farrow, Alexander.   Married Ann Obanion,
                                October 5, 1753
Frazer, William.   Son of Mary, born at Mary
                                Suddeth's, November 8, 1754
Fritter, Hugh Horton.   Son of Moses and Elizabeth,
                                born January 6, 1754
Furguson, Elizabeth.   Daughter of John, baptized
                                May 19, 1754
Flitter, John.   Married Bridget Riggins,
                                March 16, 1755

French, Rachel. Daughter of Hugh, died

January 16, 1755

Farlow, Elizabeth. Married John Burch,

August 31, 1755

Flitter, Moses. Son of Moses and Elizabeth, born

October 1, 1756

Fitzhugh, John. Was baptized February 29, 1756

Fitzhugh, Susanna. Daughter of John, was baptized

February, 25, 1756

Foxworthy, Saky. Daughter of John and Sarah, born

February 1, 1756

Frazer, Mary. Daughter of Isabella, born

June 12, 1756

Furguson, Kate. Daughter of John, baptized

October 17, 1756

Fristoe, Richard. Married Virginia Waters,

February 28, 1757

Fletcher, Moses. Married Sarah Martin,

July 10, 1757

Flitter, William. Son of Moses and Elizabeth, born

October 30, 1757

Fortick, Margaret. Married William Bradley,

March 26, 1758

Foxworthy, Thomas. Son of John, born

May 12, 1758

G.

Grant, Peter. Son of John and Margaret, born
November 18, 1739

Green, Abigail. Married Isaac Bridwell,
January 20, 1740

Gallahan, Eleanor. Daughter of John and Penelope,
born April 1, 1740

George, Elizabeth. Daughter of William and
Eleanor, born May 10, 1740

Garrison, John. Son of John and Nancy, born
May 17, 1740

Garrison, Arron. Married Elizabeth Bridwell,
May 10, 1740

Gregg, James. Son of Matthew and Catharine, born
May 18, 1740

Gregg, Elizabeth. Daughter of William, died at
William Bethel's, May 15, 1740

Garrison, Mary Anne. Daughter of Arron and
Elizabeth, born September 22, 1741

George, Elmore. Son of William, died
November 25, 1740

George, Nickolas. Married Margaret Whitson,
December 25, 1740

Green, Martha. Daughter of John and Abigail, born
April 15, 1741

Gallahan, Thomas. Son of John and Eleanor, born
March 21, 1741

Goleman, Sarah.   Daughter of Francis and Winifred,
born September 20, 1741

Griffin, Elizabeth.   Married James Philips,
September 27, 1741

Gallahan, Elizabeth.   Daughter of Solomon and
Mildred, born October 9, 1741

George, Nickolas.   Son of Nickolas and Margaret,
born November 21, 1741

Grant, William.   Son of John and Lydia, born
March 9, 1742

Garner, Parish.   Married Margaret Sturdy,
January 2, 1742

Garret, Betty.   Daughter of Robert and Mary Anne,
born May 29, 1742

Garrison, Susannah.   Daughter of John and Anne,
born May 21, 1742

George, Elmore.   Son of William and Eleanor, born
May 14, 1742

Goodwin, Jean.   Married Henry Nelson,
October 18, 1742

Garrison, George.   Son of Arron, born
November 14, 1742

Garner, James.   Son of Parish and Margaret, born
November 25, 1742

Gallahan, William.   Son of Solomon, born
April 26, 1743
Grigsby, Sarah.   Married George Fletcher,
January 1, 1743
Gough, Glady E.   Child of Thomas and Sarah, born
February 4, 1743
George, Sith.   Daughter of Benjamin and Mary, born
June 30, 1743
Gallahan, John.   Son of John and Eleanor,
July 9, 1743
Green, William.   Married Ann Robinson,
December 18, 1743
Gough, William.   Married Liny Byram,
October 19, 1743
Gough, Joshua.   Son of William and Lucy, born
March 31, 1744
Grigsby, Alice.   Married Benjamin Bush,
April 1, 1744
Garner, Thomas.   Son of Parish, born
August 25, 1744
Green, Sarah.   Daughter of Anne and William, born
September 24, 1744
Grigsby, William.   Son of John and Ann, born
October 30, 1744
Grady, William.   Son of William and Anne, born
November 11, 1744

Green, George.   Married Elizabeth Whitson,
>   December 23, 1744
Garrison, William.   Son of Mary, born
>   December 11, 1744
George, Nanny.   Daughter of Nicholas and Margaret,
>   born December 3, 1744
Gregg, John.   Son of Matthew and Catharine, born
>   December 19, 1744
Garrison, John.   Son of Aaron, born January 1, 1745
Garret, Constance.   Daughter of Robert and Mary,
>   April 3, 1745
Gowing, Isabel.   Wife of Peter, died March 11, 1745
Gallahan, Malerson.   Daughter of Solomon, born
>   May 2, 1745
Gowing, Peter and Mary Sullivant.   Married
>   May 28, 1745
Grimes, Mary.   Daughter of Richard and Elizabeth,
>   August 26, 1745
Griffin, Thomas.   Married Sarah Suddeth,
>   July 18, 1745
Garret, Daniel.   Married Mary Holliday,
>   September 4, 1745
George, William.   Married Mary Whitson,
>   November 1, 1745
Garrison, Mary.   Married John Kelly,
>   November 1, 1745

Green, Thomas. Son of George and Elizabeth, born
November 27, 1745

Grant, Jane. Married John Glendering,
January 30, 1746

Glendering, John. Married Jane Grant,
January 30, 1746

Green, Patty. Married Wiiliam Harding,
Jnauary 20, 1746

Gallahan, Solomon. Son of Mary and Solomon, born
March 26, 1747

Green, Elizabeth. Married Richard Young,
December 27, 1746

Grigsby, Priscilla. Married Abraham Fletcher,
November 28, 1746

Grigsby, Margaret. Married George Foster,
December 22, 1746

Green, Dorcas. Daughter of William and Anne, born
December 30, 1746

Garrison, William. Son of Ann, born
October 23, 1746

Griffith, Daniel. Son of Thomas and Sarah, born
September 2, 1746

Godfrey, William. Married Rebecca Robinson,
October 26, 1746

George, John. Son of William and Mary, born
March 1, 1747

Grant, Elizabeth. Daughter of John and Lydia, born
July 28, 1747
Gough, Sarah. Married William Bryan, May 14, 1747
Green, James. Married Lucy Martin, October 4, 1748
Grigsby, Susannah. Daughter of John and Ann, born
October 10, 1747
Garret, Bryan. Son of Robert and Mary, born
November 28, 1747
Grigsby, Lettie. Married Joshua Owens,
November 10, 1747
George, Elizabeth. Daughter of Nickolas and
Margaret, born December 1, 1747
Green, James. Son of John, Jr., born
January 22, 1748
Green, George. Son of George and Elizabeth, born
February 23, 1748
Garrison, Sukey. Daughter of Aaron and Elizabeth,
born March 26, 1748
Groves, Edward. Married Mary Hearne,
September 15, 1748
Garret, Bryan. Son of Robert, died
December 18, 1748
Gallahan, Alice. Daughter of John, born
December 15, 1748
Gill, Spencer. Son of Elizabeth, died
November 3, 1748

Gill, Elizabeth.   Married Joseph White,

January 31, 1749

Grace, Ellender.   Daughter of Mary, born

February 7, 1749

Groves, William.   Married Barbara Webster,

February 2, 1749

Green, Annas.   Daughter of William and Ann, born

March 18, 1749

George, Lydia.   Daughter of William and Mary, born

April 4, 1749

Gough, Sarah.   Daughter of William, born

August 15, 1749

Green, Lizzie, the wife of James, died October 29, 1749

Green, George.   Son of Lizzie and James, born

October 21, 1749

Garrison, Aaron.   Son of Aaron, born October 1, 1749

Gallahan, Mary.   Daughter of Solomon and Mary,

born January 1, 1750

Glass, Elizabeth.   Married John Lindcey.

January 15, 1750

Green, Sarah.   Daughter of John, born

January 20, 1750

George, Jane.   Married Christopher Dawson,

February 16, 1750

Grant, Ann.   Daughter of John and Lydia, born

April 8, 1750

Godfrey, Jane. Daughter of William, and Rebecca,
born February 5, 1750
Grigsby, Rachel. Daughter of John and Ann, born
August 17, 1750
Green, Sarah. Daughter of John, died August 17, 1750
Green, Daniel. Married Sarah Foxworthy,
October 16, 1750
Grinstead, Lydia. Daughter of Peter, born
January 20, 1751
Grace, Sarah. Daughter Mary, born January 8, 1751
Grey, William. Son of Ann, born January 26, 1751
Garrison, Winny. Daughter of Aaron and Elizabeth,
born April 28, 1751
Garret, Sarah. Daughter of Robert and Mary Ann,
born March 4, 1751
George, Willmouth. Daughter of Nickolas and
Margaret, born March 4, 1751
Gorman, Mary. Married James Stanard, June 20, 1751
Green, Jess. Son of John, Jr., and Jean, born
August 20, 1751
Green, Mary. Daughter of William, born
July 21, 1751
Grey, Richard. Son of John and Margaret, born
May 15, 1751
Gregg, Mathew. Married —— Chinn,
August 15, 1751

Gain, Lizzie.   Married James Matheny,
                              December 12, 1751
Green, Mary.   Married William More,
                              November 28, 1751
George, Franky.   Daughter of William and Mary,
                              born November 7, 1751
Giant, Jane.   Daughter of John and Lydia, born
                              April 17, 1752
Gough, Nanny.   Daughter of Willlam, born
                              January 29, 1752
Grant, Mary.   Wife of Jasper, died, and her child also,
                              February 27, 1752
Godfrey, James.   Son of William, born July 26, 1752
Gallahan, Charles.   Son of Solomon, born
                              May 20, 1752
Gregg, Mathew.   Son of Mathew, was baptized
                              September 17, 1752
Garrison, Sarah.   Daughter of Aaron and Elizabeth,
                              born April 24, 1753
Garret, Winifred.   Daughter of Robert and Mary,
                              born March 21, 1753
Gill, Edward.   Married Lethe Canaday
                              February 4, 1753
Grigsby, Moses.   Married Mary Matheney,
                              August 26, 1753
Grigsby, Sarah.   Married Wllliam Rose, June 5, 1753

Green, Nanny. Daughter of John, born
                              July 19, 1753
Going, Peter. Died at Priscilla Hayes',
                              May 22, 1753
Gunn, John. Married Martha Shamlin,
                              September 30, 1753
Green, Jacl. Daughter of William, born
                              November 12, 1753
Grace, John. Son of Mary, born November 4, 1753
Gaines, Frances. Daughter of Humphry and Sarah,
                              born November 14, 1753
George, Sarah Ann. Daughter of William, born
                              April 1, 1754
Green, Lizzie. Daughter of Daniel and Sarah, born
                              April 1, 1754
Gill, John. Married Elizabeth Williams,
                              March 3, 1754
Gerrard, Mary Ann. Daughter of William, baptized
                              February 17, 1754
Gerrard, Gerard. Son of Mary, born at John Waters',
                              March 14, 1755
Gashings, Isaac. Son of Sarah, born July 29, 1754
Grant, Mary. Daughter of John and Lydia, born
                              September 15, 1754
George, Sarah. Daughter of Nickolas and Margaret,
                              born October 11, 1754

Godfrey, Elizabeth.   Daughter of William and
                              Rebecca, born October 28, 1754
Gallahan, Margaret.   Daughter of Solomon, born
                                                    October 8, 1754
Grianan, Eleanor.   Married James Edzar,
                                            November 22, 1754
Gough, William.   Son of William, born
                                            February 17, 1755
Green, John.   Son of John, Jr., was born
                                                    April 4, 1755
Garrison, Moses.   Son of Aaron and Elizabeth, born
                                                    March 9, 1755
Gaines, Henry.   Son of Humphry and Sarah, born
                                                    April 11, 1755
Goolding, Susanna.   A bastard child, born
                                            March 4, 1755
Gallahan, John.   Had a daughter named Mary, born
                                            February 4, 1755
Gill, Elsy.   Daughter of John and Elizabeth, born
                                            January 28, 1755
Gwinn, James.   Married Elizabeth Maccaboy,
                                            October 5, 1755
Green, Willliam.   Son of William and Ann, born
                                                    April 28, 1756
Griffin, Phillis.   Died at James Hardwicks',
                                                    April 9, 1756

Graves, Sarah. Married George Jeffries,
>   February 8, 1756
Goldsmith, John. Married Martha Powell,
>   January 19, 1756
Grigsby, John. Son of Moses, born
>   January 18, 1756
Green, Mary. Daughter of Daniel and Sarah, born
>   August 25, 1756
Green, John. Married Phillis Smith,
>   December 19, 1756
Grogg, Sarah. Married William Brown,
>   December 11, 1756
Green, Robert. Married Helen Lowry,
>   November 23, 1756
Green, Sarah. Married Snowdall Laytham,
>   November 25, 1756
Garner, John. Son of Samuel and Isabel, born
>   November 13, 1756
George, William. Son of William, born
>   December 1, 1756
Gerrard, Anthony. Son of Jacob, baptized
>   October 12, 1756
Grant, John. Son of John and Lydia, born
>   March 11, 1756
Graham, Richard. Married Jane Brent,
>   February 10, 1757

Gallahan, Nelly.   Daughter of John, born
February 19, 1757
Gunn, Mary.   Married Robert Day, January 16, 1757
Green, William.   Son of John, born January 18, 1757
Gough, Ann.   Married William Baylis,
January 19, 1757
Gough, Peggy.   Was baptized December 23, 1757
Gerrard, Sarah.   Daughter of Mary, born
January 15, 1757
Gaines, Sarah.   Daughter of Humphrey, born
February 25, 1757
George, Lydia.   Daughter of Nickolas and Margaret,
born May 29, 1757
Grigsby, Jane.   Married William Rose,
March 14, 1758
Garrison, Milly.   Daughter of Aaron and Elizabeth,
born June 27, 1758
Greenless, Bethsheba.   Married ———, May 7, 1758
George, William.   Son of William, died June 3, 1758
Green, William.   Married Judith Harrel,
January 21, 1742

H.

Hyden, Lucy.   Daughter of William and Mary, born
December 28, 1731
Hedgman, William.   Son of Peter and Margaret,
born July 1, 1732

Hyden, Samuel. Son of William and Mary, born
June 19, 1733

Hedgman, George. Son of Peter and Margaret, born
December 11, 1734

Hyden, Henry. Son of William and Mary, born
December 2, 1735

Hyden, Charity. Daughter of William and Mary,
born June 19, 1737

Harding, William. Son of Charles and Rachel, born
March 12, 1738

Hacker, William. Married Anne Dillon,
May 21, 1738

Hamilton, Anne. Married John Alridge,
June 11, 1738

Harvie, Anne. Married Richard Wine, July 23, 1738

Humphrieys, John, Jr. Married Margaret Young,
September 23, 1738

Hays, Catharine. Married Thomas Waters,
September 28, 1738

Hammet, Margaret. Daughter of William and Mary,
born February 10, 1739

Hyden, Richard. Son of William and Mary, born
March 8, 1739

Helms, Mary. Married Gabriel Muffet, July 25, 1739

Higgerson, Hannah. Married James Whealy,
July 8, 1739

Howard, John.   Son of James and Margaret, born
September 2, 1739

Hacker, William.   Son of William, born
December 9, 1739

Hurst Jean.   Married William Bethel,
December 26, 1739

Harding, Anne.   Daughter of Charles and Rachel,
born February 3, 1740

Horton, Townshend.   Son of Snowdal and Sarah,
born April 21, 1740

Heffernon. Jane.   Married Alexander Payton,
May 20, 1740

Heffernut, Sarah.   Married William Wilkison,
August 21, 1740

Hyden, William.   Son of William and Mary, born
September 1, 1740

Hankins, Diana.   Daughter of Daniel and Hannah,
born December 8, 1740

Hurst, James.   Son of Thomas and Mary, born
November 13, 1740

Harper, Sarah.   Daughter of Mary and Michael,
born April 24, 1741

Hornbuckel, Franklin.   Son of Richard, born
April 11, 1741

Harding Wilmouth.   Daughter of Henry and
Wilmouth, born April 14, 1741

Hurst, Lauden. Son of Mary, born July 25, 1741

Heaflon, Simon. Son of William, born

October 1, 1741

Heffernon, William. Married Sarah Martin,

September 29, 1741

Hedgman, John. Son of Peter and Margaret,

born October 13, 1741

Heffernon, John. Son of James, born

November 23, 1741

Hammet, Charles. Son of William and Elizabeth,

born February 4, 1742

Harrel, Judith. Married William Green,

January 21, 1742

Higgins, John Bayham. Son of Jane, born

May 28, 1742

Holiday, Whorton. Married Elizabeth Dunest,

July 28, 1742

Harding, Jane. Daughter of Charles and Rachel,

born November 9, 1742

Hinson, Edmund. Died November 18, 1742

Hacker, John. Son of William and Anne, born

January 2, 1743

Hankins, Margaret. Daughter of Daniel and

Elizabeth, born February 6, 1743

Hickerson, John. Departed this life

February 2, 1743

Harding, Franky.   Daughter of George and Jinny,
                                    born March 7, 1743
Hyter, William.   Married Anne Hewis,
                                    April 3, 1743
Hewis, Anne.   Married William Hyter, April 3, 1743
Higerson, Sarah Elwood.   Daughter of Thomas and
                                    Sarah, born March 27, 1743
Heath, Milian.   Daughter of Thomas and Elizabeth,
                                    born January 10, 1743
Hefferton, Mary Byford.   Daughter of William, born
                                    ——, 1743
Hyden, Daniel.   Son of William and Mary, born
                                    April 6, 1743
Hill, John.   Departed this life March 19, 1743
Horton, Hoasin.   Daughter of Snowdal and Sarah,
                                    born May 16, 1743
Higgerson, Elizabeth.   Married John Waters,
                                    June 5, 1743
Harding, Nickolas.   Son of Henry and Wilmouth,
                                    born July 6, 1743
Hinston, Isabel.   Married James Felton,
                                    November 13, 1743
Homes, Henry.   Died at Anthony Murray's,
                                    November 16, 1743
Huges, Mary.   Married George Crosby,
                                    January 6, 1744

Hayter, James. Son of William and Anne, born
January 32, 1744
Hammet, Mary. Daughter of William and Elizabeth,
born February 4, 1744
Hansbrough, Peter. Son of James and Lettie, born
June 12, 1744
Hyden, Daniel. Son of William, died June 5, 1744
Hughs, James. Married Agnes MacCartee,
May 6, 1744
Hurst, Nathaniel. Son of Mary, born June 6, 1744
Holdbrook, William. Married Elizabeth King,
December 8, 1744
Hammet, Sarah. Married Christopher Roderich,
December 19, 1744
Harper, Thomas. Son of Michael and Mary, born
December 31, 1744
Hogg, John. Married Eleanor Savage,
December 19, 1744
Head, Mary. Departed this life, May 21, 1745
Hanson, Ann. Married George Bell, April 15, 1745
Hayter, Anne. Wife of William, died
March 26, 1745
Harding, Charles. Son of Charles and Rachel, born
April 6, 1745
Hose, Catharine. Married Thomas Monroe,
April 16, 1745

Hansbrough, Peter.   Married Margaret French,
February 26, 1745

Hughs, William.   Son of Agnes and James, born
February 14, 1745

Hyden, Jacob.   Son of William and Mary, born
August 18, 1745

Hornbuckle, Ann.   Married Samuel Angell,
August 14, 1745

Hurst, Priscilla.   Daughter of Thomas and Mary, born
June 21, 1745

Harding, William.   Married Patty Green,
January 28, 1746

Horton, Venus.   Daughter of Snowdel and Sarah,
born July 14, 1745

Hill, William.   Married Catharine Stacey,
September 17, 1745

Head, Charles.   Son of Mary, was born
May 13, 1745

Holliday, Mary.   Married Daniel Garret,
September 4, 1745

Hyden, William.   Son of William and Mary, died
October 21, 1745

Harvey, Elizabeth.   Married Thomas Johnson,
October 19, 1745

Horton, Anthony.   Married Rosamond Duncomb,
October 27, 1745

Harrison, Captain William.   Departed this life,
                              December 1, 1745
Hart, John.   Married Rachel Oran,
                              March 23, 1746
Holliday, Mary.   Daughter of Wharton, born
                              April 29, 1746
Hawkins, Sarah.   Daughter of Daniel, born
                              January 13, 1746
Hinson, George.   Married Margaret Burchell,
                              December 29, 1746
Hansbrough, James.   Son of James, born
                              November 11, 1746
Hansbrough, James.   Son of James and Lettie, died
                              December 14, 1746
Harding, Winny.   Daughter of George and Jean, born
                              December 1, 1746
Hunter, Elizabeth.   Married John Kenny,
                              October 12, 1746
Harding, Hall.   Son of William and Patty, born
                              October 25, 1746
Holliday, Winny.   Married James Battoo,
                              February 12, 1747
Head, Joseph.   Son of Robert and Dorothy, born
                              October 27, 1746
Horton, Reuben.   Son of Anthony and Rosamond
                              born April 27, 1747

Harper, Mary.   Daughter of Michael and Mary, born
                                February 9, 1747
Hinson, Mary.   Died at John Honey's,
                                March 16, 1747
Hughs, Agnes.   Departed this life, March 4, 1747
Higgerson, Elizabeth.   Married Samuel Elliot,
                                May 20, 1747
Hornbuckle, Richard.   Departed this life,
                                July 29, 1747
Horton, Francis.   Daughter of Elizabeth, born
                                June 21, 1747
Harrison, Thomas.   Married Ann Peyton,
                                July 2, 1747
Harding, John Scott.   Son of Charles and Rachel,
                                born August 3, 1747
Hansbrough, William.   Son of Peter, born
                                August 4, 1747
Hurst, John.   Died the sixth day of December, 1747
Hornbuckle, Elizabeth.   Married John Smith,
                                December 31, 1747
Holliday, John.   Son of Wharton and Elizabeth, born
                                January 11, 1747
Horton, George.   A bastard of Mary Horton, born
                                January 26, 1748
Honey, John.   Married Hannah Bussel,
                                February 2, 1748

Husk, Hanny.   Daughter of Thomas and Mary, born
January 24, 1748

Hansbrough, Elizabeth Magdalene.   Daughter of Lillie
and James, born February 22, 1748

Herrod, John.   Married Mary Devane,
August 21, 1748

Hearne, Mary.   Married Edward Groves,
September 15, 1748

Hayes, Mary.   Married Richard Fristoe,
December 24, 1748

Hinson, Mary.   Married Henry Threlkeld,
November 2, 1748

Hurst, Mary.   Married Owen Wingfield,
November 26, 1748

Hammet, Robert.   Married Lythe Bethel,
February 7, 1749

Hawes, Samuel.   Married Mary Ann Bails,
February 16, 1749

Harding, Ann.   Daughter of George and Jane, born
May 29, 1749

Horton, Aden.   Son of Anthony and Rosamond, born
June 4, 1749

Hampton, Thomas.   Married Sarah Pattison alais
Congers, January 1, 1749

Harding, Thomas.   Son of Charles and Rachel, born
August 11, 1749

Horton, William.   Married Margaret Cooke,
                                    December 21, 1749
Herrod, William.   Son of John, born
                                    December 13, 1749
Hore, Elias.   Son of Elias and Mary, born
                                    December 31, 1749
Holliday, Keziah.   Married Robert Million,
                                    December 14, 1749
Hyden, Nathaniel.   Was born December 1, 1749
Horton, John.   Son of Sarah and John, born
                                    December 23, 1749
Harper, Margaret.   Was baptized December 3, 1749
Haffermon, James.   Son of James, born
                                    September 20, 1749
Hammet, William.   Son of Robert and Sith, born
                                    November 14, 1749
Hunter, John.   Died at Captain Wm. Mountjoy's,
                                    September 29, 1749
Hornbuckle, George.   Died at John Smith's
                                    September 10, 1749
Hurst, Henry.   Married Ann Pyke, March 20, 1750
Hinson, Charles.   Departed this life,
                                    February 22, 1750
Hinson, Joyie.   Married James Crap, June 3, 1750
Hinson, Lettie.   Daughter of George, born
                                    May 21, 1750

Harod, Margaret. Daughter of Mary, Surnamed
                              Deveene, February 6, 1750
Hurst, Absolum. Son of Thomas, born
                              May 15, 1750
Horton, Benjamin. Son of Martha, born
                              August 26, 1750
Hansbrough, Milly. Daughter of James, born
                              May 5, 1750
Harrison, Susannah. Married Robert Slaughter,
                              December 11, 1750
Hardwick, Haswel. Married Mary Northcut,
                              December 8, 1750
Harvey, Milly. Married John Angell,
                              October 5, 1750
Horton, Thomas. Son of Mary, born January 4, 1750
Hurst, James. Married Rosannah Jones,
                              April 21, 1751
Hurst, Nancy. Daughter of Henry, born
                              April 20, 1751
Horton, Mary. Daughter of William, born
                              March 22, 1751
Howard, Grace. Departed this life, February 7, 1751
Hope, Samuel. Died at Alexander Nelson's,
                              April 24, 1751
Howard, William. Married Elizabeth Stacey,
                              May 29, 1751

Horton, Elizabeth.   Married Moses Fritter,
                              December 1, 1751
Hall, Mary.   Married Charles Wawal,
                              November 16, 1751
Hose, Betty.   Daughter of Elias and Mary, born
                              October 6, 1751
Hill, John.   Son of William and Catharine, born
                              October 11, 1751
Hyden, Mary.   Married John Nicholson,
                              April 23, 1752
Horton, Anthony.   Died at the house of Hugh
                              Horton's, September 21, 1751
Harper, Phobe.   Daughter of Michael and Mary, born
                              March 13, 1752
Harding, Moses.   Son of Charles and Rachel, born
                              March 19, 1752
Hazel, Fanny.   Daughter of P. Hazel, born
                              January 18, 1752
Hurst, Elizabeth.   Daughter of James and Rosamond,
                              born January 10, 1752
Howard, Elizabeth.   Daughter of William and
                              Elizabeth, born August 14, 1752
Honey, William.   Son of John, baptized
                              July 19, 1752
Holliday, Mary.   Daughter of Wharton, born
                              June 9, 1752

Hansbrough, Peter.   Married Lydia Smith,

May 27, 1752

Hinson, Margaret.   Wife of George, died

November 22, 1752

Hinson, Mary.   Daughter of George and Margaret,

born October 28, 1752

Hansbrough, Gabriel.   Son of James, born

November 17, 1752

Horton, Phobe.   Daughter of John and Sarah, born

March 14, 1752

Hinson, Elizabeth.   Daughter of Sarah, born

May 31, 1753

Hyden, Daniel.   Born at his home, March 17, 1753

Hardwick, Ann.   Daughter of Hasel and Mary, born

January, 4, 1752

Horton, Dunnel.   Son of William and Margaret, born

January 4, 1753

Hinson, George.   Married Sarah Sullivan,

February 4, 1753

Harding, Henry.   Son of George and Jane, born

August 29, 1753

Hill, William.   Son of William, born August 4, 1753

Hill, Martha.   Daughter of James and Lydia, born

May 5, 1753

Hansbrough, Smith.   Son of Peter and Lydia, born

June 30, 1753

Hughes, Elizabeth.   Daughter of Ralph, born
June 30, 1753
Hurst, Henry.   Son of James and Rosanna, born
December 3, 1753
Hardwick, William.   Son of Hasel and Mary, born
September 5, 1753
Hughes, Doffus.   Died at Mary Suddeth's,
September 14, 1753
Hill, Martha.   Married James Bussel, February 24, 1754
Hedgman, Margaret.   Wife of Peter, died
January 16, 1754
Holdbrook, Elizabeth.   Married Samuel Earle,
January 13, 1754
Horton, Winifred.   Daughter of Martha, born
July 28, 1754
Harding, George.   Son of Charles and Rachel, born
July 31, 1754
Hinson, Elizah.   Son of George and Sarah, born
May 27, 1754
Horton, Orpan.   Daughter of John and Sarah, born
February 14, 1754
Hamilton, Henry.   Was baptized February 24, 1754
Haynie, Winifred.   Daughter of Charles and Elizabeth,
born February 12, 1754
Holdbrook, Elizabeth.   Married James Cinberford,
September 15, 1754

Harding, Ann.   Departed this life,

> September 13, 1754

Hutt, Aggy.   Married William Ticer,

> December 15, 1754

Holliday, Jannie.   Daughter of Wharton, born

> September 22, 1754

Hill, George.   Son of William and Catharine, born

> February 19, 1755

Heath, Susanna Thomson.   Married John Richards,

> March 6, 1755

Humphreys, Franky.   Daughter of William and Sarah,

> born March 8, 1755

Horton, Snowdal.   Departed this life,

> January 19, 1755

Higgison, Thomas.   Died at John Water's

> February 21, 1755

Heckeney, Dianah.   Departed this life,

> January 25, 1755

Hammet, William.   Married Rosamond Smith,

> May 6, 1755

Horton, Phobe.   Daughter of John, died

> July 17, 1755

Horton, Orpha.   Daughter of John and Sarah, died

> August 8, 1755

Howard, Elizabeth.   Wife of William, died

> July 12, 1755

Honey, John.   Son of John and Hannah, born
                              July 31, 1755
Hainsford, Stephen.   Married Margaret MacCarthy,
                              October 14, 1755
Hainsbrough, James.   Son of James, born
                              October 30, 1755
Hardwick, Elizabeth   Daughter of Hasel and Mary,
                              born September 8, 1755
Hayes, Priscilla.   Daughter of Thomas, baptized
                              November 28, 1755
Hinson, Sarah.   Daughter of Lazarus and Sarah, born
                              November 21, 1755
Hay, Priscilla.   Daughter of Thomas and Frances,
                              born November 8, 1755
Hore, Nathaniel Brown.   Son of Elias, born
                              December 18, 1755
Hyden, William.   Was born January 28, 1756
Hamilton, Leanna.   Daughter of Henry, born
                              February 2, 1756
Howard, William.   Married Martha Wheeler,
                              April 25, 1756
Hansbrough, Sarah.   Daughter of Lydia and Peter,
                              born March 13, 1756
Harding, Ann.   Married Mark Waters, July 20, 1756
Hunt, Milly.   Daughter of James and Rosanna, born
                              August 26, 1756

Hughes, John. Son of Ralph, born
December 24, 1756
Harrison, Sarah. Married John Monroe,
September 23, 1756
Hore, Samuel Brown. Son of Elias, baptized
February 8, 1756
Hedgman, George. Married Hannah Daniel,
November 27, 1756
Horton, Beverly. Son of William and Margaret, born
April 8, 1757
Hall, Lettie. Daughter of John, born March 2, 1757
Harrison, Margaret. Married Edward Blackburn,
May 26, 1757
Holliday, Betty. Daughter of Wharton, born
June 27, 1757
Hay, Catharine. Daughter of Thomas and Frances,
born October 12, 1757
Horton, Clara. Daughter of John and Sarah, born
December 5, 1757
Hurst, James. Son of Thomas and Mary, born
March 19, 1757
Harding, Sarah. Daughter of Jean and George, born
March 26, 1758
Horton, Martha. Married Peter Byram,
March 23, 1758
Hord, Mary. Married ———, 1758

Helms, Sarah. Daughter of Samuel, born
                                                    May 25, 1758
Halley, William. Married Catharine Jeffries,
                                                    February 9, 1758
Hansbrough, Anna Violet. Daughter of James, born
                                                    April 24, 1758
Hurst, Elijah. Son of John, born February 16, 1758
Hammond, Charles. Son of John and Elizabeth, born
                                                    April 20, 1758
Higgerson, John. Married Jean Jackson,
                                                    January 20, 1741-2

I.

Isaac, Margaret. Married Alexander Suitor,
                                                    July 21, 1754
Innis, James. Son of John and Mary, born
                                                    March 11, 1752
Innis, James. Was baptized April 12, 1752
Innis, William. Son of John and Mary, born
                                                    July 9, 1757

J.

Johnston, Benoin. Son of William and Frances, born
                                                    February 4, 1740
Judd, Mary. The daughter of ———, died
                                                    May 23, 1740

Johnston, Silent. Married John Simpson,
                                    August 17, 1740
Jackson, Sarah. Daughter of John and Sarah, born
                                    November 2, 1740
Jackson, Jean. Married John Higgerson,
                                    January 20, 1741–2
Jones, George. Son of John and Mary, born
                                    March 3, 1741
Jeffries, Alexander. Married Lettie Burton,
                                    September 30, 1741
Jackson, Henry. Son of William and Grace, born
                                    October 8, 1741
Jones, Elizabeth Warner. Daughter of Briviton and
                                    Lettie, born October 7, 1741
Johnston, Wilmouth. Daughter of William and
                                    Frances, born May 17, 1742
Jeffries, Alexander. Had a child named ———, born
                                    September 6, 1742
Jones, John. Son of John and Mary, born
                                    October 10, 1742
James, Margaret. Daughter of George, baptized
                                    November 21, 1742
Jenkins, Sarah. Married William Corbin,
                                    January 1, 1743
Jack, Jean. Married Matthew Brooks,
                                    February —, 1743

Jeffries, Silent. Married Rose Suthard,

January 19, 1744

Jones, Sarah. Married William Matheney,

March 22, 1743–4

Tudd, Jean. Married Daniel Dunaway, March 1, 1744

Jackson, Sith. Was born March 23, 1744

Jones, Robert. Son of Breveton and Lettie, born

June 29, 1754

Jeffries, James. Son of Alexander, born

November 25, 1744

Jones, Elizabeth. Married Robert Bridwell,

January 13, 1745

Johnson, Thomas. Married Elizabeth Harvey,

October 19, 1745

Jones, Thomas. Married Frances Leftridge,

(Leftwich,) December 16, 1746

Jeffries, James. Married Sarah Matthews,

December 23, 1746

James, Joseph. Son of George and Mary, born

December 8, 1746

Jones, James. Married Frances Mason,

January 8, 1747

Jeffries, Susannah. Daughter of James and Elizabeth,

born April 8, 1747

Jeffries, Betty. Daughter of James and Sarah, born

August 11, 1747

Jeffries, Betty. Departed this life, August 17, 1747

Jones, Eliza. Son of Thomas and Frances, born
September 22, 1747

Jones, Rose. Married John Robertson,
October 15, 1747

Jordan, Willoughby. Son of William and Sarah, born
May 8, 1748

Jeffries, Catharine. Daughter of James, born
October 25, 1747

James, Daniel. Son of George, born
December 6, 1748

James, Margaret. Daughter of George, died
October 30, 1748

James, William. Departed this life November 2, 1748

James, Hannah. Married Benjamin Crump,
February 2, 1749

Jackson, William. Departed this life, March 16, 1749

Jackson, Dianna. Daughter of William and Jane,
born May 9, 1749

Jordon, Nanny. Married William Foster,
June 15, 1749

Jones, Catharine. Married Thomas Barry,
August 5, 1749

Jackson, John. Son of Grace, born April —, 1750

Jenkins, Mary. Married John Cubbage, July 10, 1750

Johnston, Archibald. Was baptized October 21, 1750

Jones, Rosannah.   Married James Hurst,
                                 April 21, 1751
Jones, Charles.   Married Elizabeth Sinclair,
                                 April 21, 1751
Jennings, Martha.   Married Thomas Asbury,
                                 December 1, 1751
Jeffries, Elizabeth.   Married Nelson Kelly,
                        November 4, 1751, by Mr. Macdonal
Johnston, William.   Died at John Prim's
                                 December 25, 1751
Jordan, Mary.   Married Nicholas Foxworthy,
                                 January 26, 1752
Jones, John.   Married Margaret Jenkins,
                                 November 26, 1752
Jenkins, Margaret.   Married John Jones,
                                 November 26, 1752
Johnson, Elizabeth.   Departed this life,
                                 November 13, 1752
Jones, Phillis.   Married William Sturdy,
                                 December 17, 1752
Johnson, Rachel.   Was born October 23, 1752
Jackson, John.   Son of Grace, died March 15, 1753
Jeffries, Lydia.   Daughter of James and Sarah, born
                                 September 17, 1754
Jackson, Grace.   Died at John Peyton's,
                                 September 17, 1754

Jeffries, Joseph.   Married Margaret Smith,
                               October 24, 1754
Johns, Jane.   Daughter of Elizabeth, born
                               March 16, 1755
Jack, Mary.   Married Simon Robinson,
                               August 3, 1755
Jeffries, Sarah.   Daughter of Joseph and Margaret,
                               born August 22, 1755
Jones, Mary.   Daughter of John, born
                               October 4, 1755
Johnson, Eleanor.   Daughter of William and Tabitha,
                               born December 8, 1755
Jeffries, George.   Married Sarah Graves,
                               February 8, 1756
Jeffries, Sarah.   Daughter of James, baptized
                               April 25, 1756
Jeffries, Catharine.   Married William Halley,
                               February 9, 1758

K.

King, William.   Married Elizabeth Edward,
                               May 21, 1738
King, John.   Son of William and Elizabeth, born
                               December 1, 1740
Kenton, Mary,   Daughter of Mark and Mary, born
                               August 9, 1740

Kendal, Jesse. Son of William, Jr., born
                          November 4, 1740
Kirke, John. Married Sarah Robinson, June 23, 1741
Kirke, Winifred. Daughter of John and Sarah, born
                          April 21, 1742
Kinny, Richard. Son of James, born April 9, 1742
Kendal, Thomas. Son of William and Jemima, born
                          March 27, 1742
Kemp, John. Son of James and Elizabeth, born
                          August 28, 1742
Kirke, John Hardy. Son of Sarah, born
                          March 30, 1743
Kirke, Sarah. The wife of William, died
                          December 28, 1743
Knight, Nelly. Daughter of Leanod and Nelly, born
                          August 7, 1743
Kenny, William. Son of James and Ann, born
                          December 22, 1743
Kendal, George. Son of William and Jemima, born
                          January 13, 1744
Knight, Mary Ann. Daughter of Christopher, born
                          June 14, 1744
King, Elizabeth. Married William Holdbrook,
                          December 8, 1744
Kenny, Andrew. Married Ann Clarnes,
                          November 30, 1744

Knight, John. Married Charity Latimore,
                                    October 23, 1750
Kendal, Jesse. Departed this life, November 18, 1740
Kirke, Randale. Son of the said John and Sarah,
                                    born April 21, 1742
Kirk, William. Son of Sarah, born June 6, 1742
Kirke, Winifred. The daughter of John and Sarah,
                                    born April 21, 1742
Knight, George. Married Jean Dawson,
                                    December 25, 1744
Kirke, John. Son of John and Sarah, born
                                    January 20, 1745
King, William. Son of William and Elizabeth, born
                                    February 22, 1745
Kendal, James. Married Mary Coffey,
                                    February 25, 1745
Kenny, Nancy. Daughter of Andrew and Anne, born
                                    October 15, 1745
Kendal, Anne. Daughter of William and Jemima,
                                    born December 6, 1745
Kenny, Thomas. Son of James and Anne, born
                                    August 2, 1745
Kelly, John. Married Mary Garrison,
                                    November 1, 1745
Knight, Elizabeth. Daughter of George and Jean,
                                    born March 4, 1745–6

Knight, William.   Son of Elizabeth, born
                                February 28, 1745–6
Kenny, John.   Married Elizabeth Hunter,
                                October 12, 1746
King, Weathers.   Son of William, died
                                August 20, 1747
Kirke, Elijah.   Son of John and Sarah, born
                                July 2, 1747
Kendal, Jesse.   Son of James and Mary, born
                                June 19, 1747
Kenny, Calib.   Son of John and Mary, born
                                May 21, 1747
Kelly, Honour.   Died at William Wright's,
                                August 13, 1747
Knight, John.   Son of George, born October 22, 1747
Knight, William.   Departed this life
                                November 27, 1747
Kirke, Elijah.   Son of John, died November 25, 1747
Kitchen, Richard.   Son of James and Mary, born
                                January 18, 1748
Kendal, John.   Son of William and Jemima, born
                                March 21, 1748
Kendall, William.   Married Jemimah Kirk,
                                May 10, 1748
Kirk, Jemimah.   Married William Kendall,
                                May 10, 1748

Kendal, George. Married Margaret Kelly,
June 5, 1748
Kelly, Margaret. Married George Kendal,
June 5, 1748
Kendal, Joshua. Married Catharine Smith,
April 4, 1749
Kendall, John. Son of James and Mary, born
February 26, 1749
Knight, Elizabeth. Married Nicholas Bennet,
June 12, 1749
Kenny, Sarah. Daughter of James and Ann, born
April 15, 1749
Kenny, Elizabeth. Daughter of Andrew and Ann,
born August 30, 1749
Kendal, William and Samuel. Sons of William and
Jemimah, born August 30, 1749
Kendall, Jess. Son of James, died April 17, 1750
Kendall, Henry. Was baptized March 4, 1750
Kitchen, Merryman. Son of James, born
March 26, 1750
King, Nimrod. Son of William, born
November 29, 1750
Kelly, Sarah. Married William Sebastian,
June 11, 1751
Kirke, Laricha. Daughter of John and Sarah, born
May 8, 1751

Kendal, Jess. Son of Joshua, born August 21, 1751

Knight, Samuel. Son of John and Charity, born
August 15, 1751

King, Josiah. Married Martha Fristoe,
December 12, 1751

Kelly, Nelson. Married Elizabeth Jeffries,
November 14, 1751

Kenny, Reuben. Son of James and Ann, born
October 12, 1751

Kendal, John. Married Catharine Kees,
January 9, 1752

Kees, Catharine. Married John Kendal,
January 9, 1752

King, Martha. Married Joseph MacCollough,
February 9, 1752

Kendrick, James. Son of Patrick and Jane, born
January 10, 1752

Kitchen, Elizabeth. Daughter of James and Mary,
born January 15, 1748

Kendal, Mary Ann. Daughter of William and
Jemima, born April 9, 1752

Kendon, Edward. Married Mary Waller,
April 15, 1753

Kirke, William. Departed this life March 21, 1753

Kendal, Samuel. Son of John and Catharine, born
January 1, 1753

Kendal, Joshua. Son of Joshua and Catharine, born
May 27, 1753
Kirke, Sarah. Daughter of John and Sarah, born
September 5, 1753
Knight, Sarah Ann. Daughter of George and Jean,
born October 2, 1753
Kendal, Lizzie. Daughter of William and Jemima,
born April 1, 1754
Knight, Ephraim. Son of Isaac, born
February 3, 1754
Kite, John. Son of John, was baptized, July 14, 1754
Kendal, Charles. Son of John and Catharine, born
September 7, 1754
Kendrick, Isabel. Daughter of Patrick and Jane, born
October 13, 1754
Kenny, Mary Ann. Was born January 9, 1755
Kirke, Elizabeth. Daughter of John, born
November 24, 1755
Kendal, Bailey. Son of James and Mary, born
October 8, 1755
King, Elizabeth. Daughter of William, baptized
September 7, 1755
Kendal, Nancy. Daughter of Joshua and Catharine,
born December 19, 1755
Kennedy, Jane. Daughter of Milly, born
March 29, 1756

Kennedy, Isabel. Married William Patten,
                                December 19, 1756
Kirk, Henry. Married Sarah Lunsford,
                                May 23, 1756
Knight, Peter. Married Rachel Abbot,
                                December 19, 1756
Kirk, Suky. Daughter of Henry and Sarah, born
                                April 25, 1757
King, John Edwards. Son of William, born
                                December 21, 1757
Knight, Christopher. Son of Peter and Rachel, born
                                November 7, 1757
Knight, Ephram. Married Ann Abbot,
                                born February 12, 1758
Kendal, Elizabeth. Daughter of John and Catharine,
                                born February 11, 1758
Kendal, Betty. Daughter of Joshua and Catharine,
                                born February 22, 1758
Kendal, Jeremiah. Son of William and Jemima, born
                                February 6, 1758

L.

Lewis, Walter Morgan. Married Mary Abram,
                                August 27, 1738
Limbrick, Susannah. Daughter of William, born
                                October 12, 1739

Lamb, Mary. Married Edward Malphus,

December 25, 1740

Linton, Mary. Married John Remy, April 6, 1740

Lowry, Judith. Daughter of William and Tabitha,

born February 13, 1742

Lunsford, Sarah. Daughter of William and Mary,

born March 7, 1744

Luns, Letty. Daughter of Bebina, born June 21, 1744

Latimore, Mary. Married Lewis Pritchet,

March 4, 1744

Lunsford, Hannah. Daughter of William and

Dinah, born June 5, 1744

Limbrick, James. Son of William and Catharine,

born May 10, 1744

Lawless, Thomas. Son of Mary, born

January 28, 1744

Lawless, Thomas. Son of Mary, died

September 10, 1744

Lowry, George. Son of William and Tabitha, born

November 24, 1744

Latham, Mary. Married Henry Suddeth,

June 25, 1745

Lee, Joseph. Married Mary Bethel,

November 14, 1745

Latham, Jane, Died at Mary Richard's,

January 7, 1745–6

Leftridge, Frances. Married Thomas Jones,
December 16, 1746
Lunsford, Charlotte. Daughter of William and
Dinah, born December 26, 1746
Latham, Frances. Departed this life, October 2, 1746
Latham, John. Departed this life, October 1, 1746
Lunsford, Mary. Daughter of William, born
September 7, 1746
Lowry, Tabitha. Married Jeremiah Stark,
January 29, 1747
Lunsford, Rebecca. Married John Baker,
June 8, 1747
Linee, Margaret. Married William Cannaday,
January 16, 1747
Lemmon, John. Married Eleanor McCarty,
April 10, 1748
Lymm, Joseph. Son of Rose, born March 24, 1748
Limon, James. Son of John, born August 15, 1748
Limbrich, Rachel. Married Thomas Porch,
July 22, 1748
Lacy, Sarah. Married Rawleigh Chinn,
September 2, 1748
Lunsford, Benjamin. Son of William, born
February 10, 1749
Limbrick, Vinson. Son of William, died
April 28, 1749

Lincey, John. Married Elizabeth Glass,

> January 15, 1750

Lunsford, Judith. Married John Petter,

> February 27, 1750

Lymm, Frank. Son of Rose, was born

> April 21, 1751

Latimore, Charity. Married John Knight,

> October 23, 1750

Lunsford, Hannah. Daughter of William, born

> October 16, 1751

Latham, Sarah. Married William Mays,

> February 9, 1752

Lemaster, Elizabeth. Daughter of Thomas and

> Lettie, born January 14, 1753

Lunsford, Rowley. Married Joanna Sturdy,

> June 16, 1754

Lunsford, Alice. Married Joshua Brown,

> July 21, 1754

Lynah, Margaret. Daughter of Rose, born at

> Peter Ront's, July 23, 1754

Linton, Lettie. Married Joseph Carter,

> February 5, 1755

Lunsford, Jane. Daughter of Moses and Rachel,

> born April 24, 1756

Lunsford Lettie. Married William Simpson,

> January 18, 1756

Lunsford, John.   Married Margaret Martyn,
                                January 6, 1756
Lunsford, Sarah.   Married Henry Kirk,
                                May 23, 1756
Lewis, Zackias.   Married Mary Brent,
                                August 24, 1756
Lowry, Helen.   Married Robert Green,
                                November 23, 1756
Laytham, Snowdall.   Married Sarah Green,
                                November 28, 1756
Laytham, Jemima.   Daughter of Snowdall and Sarah,
                                born November 7, 1758
Lea, Lucy.   Married ———— Bridwell,
                                April 9, 1758
Lunsford, Susanna.   Married John Peyton,
                                March 28, 1758
Lane, James.   Married Mary Smith,
                                January 12, 1758
Lunsford, Enoch.   Son of John, born
                                born February 28, 1758
Lane, James Hardage.   Married Mary Smith,
                                January 12, 1758
Lyon, Margaret.   Married John Abbot,
                                January 15, 1758
Lynns, Margaret.   Married Thomas Darlow,
                                April 9, 1758

M.

Mercer, Mason. Son of John and Catharine, born
July 2 and died July 23, 1720

Mercer, John. Son of John and Catharine, born
December 17, 1727

Murray, John. Son of John and Mary, born
March 1, 1729

Mercer, Elizabeth Mason. Daughter of John and
Catharine, born February 16, 1730

Mercer, Elizabeth Mason. Daughter of John and
Catharine, died August 31, 1732

Mercer, John. Son of John and Catharine, died
September 12, 1730

Mercer, George. Son of John and Catharine, born
July 2, 1733

Mercer, John Fenton. Son of John and Catharine,
born August 31, 1735

Mercer, James. Son of John and Catharine, born
February 26, 1736–7

Mountjoy, Edward. Son of William and Phillis, his
wife, born January 1, 1736

Mountjoy, William. Son of William and Phillis, born
Sepember 28, 1737

Mercer, Sarah Ann Mason. Daughter of John and
Catharine, born June 21, 1738

Mcinteer, Sarah. Married Andrew Davison,
November 5, 1738

Murray, Sarah. Daughter of Anthony, born
February 24, 1739

Miller, William. Married Anne Dono,
March 5, 1738–9

Mathews, Elizabeth. Married Timothy Oneal,
April 22, 1739

Muffet, Gabriel. Married Mary Helms,
July 25, 1739

Markham, Margaret. Married Taylor Chapman,
September 13, 1739

McDuell, William. Married Sarah Chambers,
December 26, 1739

Miller, Anne. Daughter of William and Ann, born
December 23, 1739

Manzey, John. Son of Peter and Elizabeth, born
December 17, 1739

Matheny, Mary. Married Edward Ponton,
November 20, 1739

McDaniel, Mary. Daughter of James and Martha,
born January 6, 1740

McInteer, Joyie. Married William Patten,
January 27, 1740

Manzey, Jemima. Daughter of John and Hester, born
March 26, 1740

Masters, Mary. Daughter of Jared and Anne, born
May 4, 1740

Moyon, Rosamond. Married Stephen Phips,
June 1, 1740

Mercer, Mary. Daughter of John and Catharine, born
August 23, 1740

McDonald, Rev. Daniel. Married Ellen Barret,
July 28, 1740

McDuell, John. Son of William and Sarah, born
June 22, 1740

Mousley, James. Died at Major Peter Hedgman's
June 8, 1740

Mason, Anne. Daughter of Willam and Mary, died
August 20, 1740

Miller, Simon. Married Isabella Miller,
October 2, 1740

Miller, Isabella. Married Simon Miller,
October 2, 1740

Murray, James. Son of Anthony and Mary, died
September 26, 1740

Murphy, John. Son of Gabriel and Mary, born
September 6, 1740

Murray; Anthony. Son of Anthony and Mary, died
October 4, 1740

Malphus, Edward. Married Mary Lamb,
December 28, 1740

Million, William.   Son of Robert, died
December 5, 1740
More, Elizabeth.   Daughter of Jonathan and Elizabeth,
born December 20, 1740
Murray, Sarah.   Daughter of Anthony and Mary, died
November 17, 1740
Morris, Anne.   Daughter of Anne and John, born
November 14, 1740
Million, Elizabeth.   Daughter of Robert, died
December 7, 1740
Monk, Robert.   Departed this life, January 31, 1741
Merriman. Mary.   Daughter of Adrian or Adam and
Elizabeth, born January 19, 1741
Martin, Francis.   Son of Francis and Betty, born
February, 25, 1741
Montjoy, Jonathan.   Son of Thomas and Elizabeth,
born February 28, 1741
Morris, Margaret.   Daughter of Griffen and Elizabeth,
born February 10, 1741
Moncure.   The Rev. Mr. John Moncure of this Parish
was married to Miss Frances Brown, oldest
daughter of Dr. Gustavus Brown, of Charles
County, Maryland, June 18, 174] · *1741*
Mason, Mary.   Married Thomas Butler, April 7, 1741
Mallaken, Mary.   Married Joseph Williams,
February 9, 1741

Million, Anne.   Daughter of Robert and Grace, died
April 8, 1741
McCarty, John. Son of William and Agnes, born·
March 27, 1741
McCarty, James.   Son of John, born April 1, 1741
Milliner, Elizabeth.   Married James Campbell,
September 27, 1741
Marten, Sarah.   Married William Heffermon,
September 29, 1741
Mountjoy, Thomas.   Son of William and Phillis,
born October 24, 1740
Mason, Lewis.   Son of William, born
October 28, 1741
Murray, John.   Son of Anthony, born
October 9, 1741
Mountjoy, John.   Son of William and Phillis, born
October 25, 1741
Murphy, Mary.   Died at Edward Malphus',
October 1, 1741
McGuirk, John.   Married Rachel Wade,
December 23, 1741
Matthews, Philip   Married Catharine Cossity,
January 4, 1742
Murray, Anthony.   Departed this life, October 4, 174C
Mercer, Thomson Mason.   Son of John and Catharine,
born April 9, 1740

Mathews, Catharine. Daughter of Samuel and Anne,
born March 5, 1742

Murphy, Matthew. Son of John and Elizabeth, born
August 17, 1742

Montgomery, Sarah. Wife of John, died
August 30, 1742

Marten, James. Married Sarah Dunaway,
January 22, 1741

Minor, Nicholas. Son of James, was born
June 4, 1742

Martin, Jean. Daughter of Thomas and Sarah, born
June 6, 1742

McDuell, Mary. Daughter of William and Sarah,
born May 4, 1742

Monk, Priscilla. Daughter of Elizabeth, born
May 7, 1742

Makanes, Samuel. Married Fransisme Cravens,
November 14, 1742

Mannel, Elizabeth. Married Arthur Dent,
December 11, 1742

McColin, Mary. Daughter of John, born
December 30, 1742

Minor, Allender. Daughter of John and Margaret,
born January 10, 1742

McDonald, William. Son of Martha and James, born
January 25, 1742

Morris, John. Son of Griffen and Elizabeth, born
January 22, 1742

Malphus, Mary. Departed this life a few days after
her husband on the 19th of October, ——

Malphus, Edward. Departed this life,
September 15, 1743

Mitchel, Elizabeth. Daughter of Jedidiah, born
September 18, 1743

Murray, Nancy. Daughter of Anthony, born
October 8, 1743

Manzey, Priscilla. Married William Rassan,
October 27, 1743

Mountjoy, Mary. Daughter of William and Phillis
born November 6, 1743

McCarty, William. Departed this life,
September 15, 1743

More, Nathaniel. Married Elee Nickolas,
December 31, 1743

Montgomery, John. Married Mary Smith,
January 16, 1744

Molton, George. Married Margaret Strother,
April 6, 1744

Martin, Charles. Son of Francis and Elizabeth, born
April 22, 1744

MacFarlane, Priscilla. Daughter of Daniel, born
April 10, 1744

Matheny, William.   Married Sarah Jones,

March 22, 1744

More, John.   Son of Nathaniel, born

August 1, 1744

Monk, Elizabeth.   Married William Walker,

May 23, 1744

Moncure, Frances.   The wife of the Rev. John Moncure,
was delivered of a son about 20 minutes
after ten at night, and was privately baptized by the Rev. James Scott about two
hours after by the name of John, and
departed this life next morning about six
of the clock, in the year 1744, and the
month July 13

Moncure, Frances.   The wife of the Rev. John Moncure, was delivered of a daughter about 35
minutes after 4 o'clock in the afternoon
the 17th day of October, 1748, and baptized
December 2d by the Rev. James Scott,
who, with George Mason, Esq., were God
Fathers; Miss Mary Mason and Elizabeth
Brown, her God Mothers, and called Ann
(see July, 1741)

MacCartee, Agnes.   Married James Hughs,

May 6, ·1744

Moncure, Frances.   Wife of the Rev. John Moncure,

was delivered of a son about half an hour
after four in the morning, January 7,
1746–7, and baptized John, March 3, 1747,
by the Rev. Mr. John Phipps; John Mercer
and George Macon, Esq., his God Fathers,
and Elizabeth Brown, his Aunt, his God
Mother

Moncure, Frances. The wife of the Rev. John Moncure, was delivered of a daughter about
fifty minutes past ten in the forenoon,
September 20, 1745, and baptized Frances
by the Rev. James Scott, September 28,
1745. He and George Mason (Gents.),
her God Fathers; Mrs. Anne Carter, the
wife of Charles Carter, Esq., and Mrs.
Sarah Scott, her God Mothers

Mathews, John. Son of William, Jr., aged six years,
died November 11, 1744

Manzey, Henry. Married Ann Withers,
November 11, 1744

MacCoy, Elizabeth. Daughter of Murdy and Ann,
born September 29, 1744

More, Mary. An orphan, died at John Water's,
November 10, 1744

Monroe, Thomas. Married Catharine Hore,
April 16, 1745

Morris, William.   Son of Griffin and Elizabeth, born
June 20, 1745

Massey, Thomas.   Married Eleanor Perender,
June 26, 1745

Moore, Nathaniel.   Married Sarah Page,
September 11, 1745

Million, Winifred.   Married Elias Ashby,
September 4, 1745

Mason, Lewis.   Son of William, died
October 29, 1745

Morris, Mary.   Married John Smith,
December 26, 1745

Manzey, Elizabeth.   Daughter of Peter, born
December 20, 1745

Murray, Lettie.   Daughter of Anthony and Mary,
born December 23, 1745

Moore, Sarah.   Daughter of Nathaniel and Sarah,
born November 6, 1745

Matthis, Richard.   Married Mary Plummer,
October 5, 1745

Million, Charky.   Daughter of Robert, baptized
December 15, 1745

Matheny, Daniel, had two of his family to die,
November 4 and 24, 1745

Moussby, Anne.   Died at William Mason's,
November 3, 1745

Montjoy, Alvin. Son of William and Phillis, was
baptized February 9, 1746

Mitchel, John. Son of Jedidiah and Lydia, was
baptized April 6, 1746

Moss, Prisby. Son of Sylvester and Elizabeth, born
May 24, 1746

Montgomery, Jane. Daughter of John, born
August 20, 1746

Mathews, Sarah. Married James Jeffries,
December 23, 1746

Mason, Margaret. Married Joseph Carter,
November 27, 1746

Mason, Elizabeth. Departed this life,
November 5, 1746

Mason, Frances. Married James Jones,
January 8, 1747

Monroe, George Hore. Son of Thomas and Catharine,
born September 3, 1747

Mason, John. Married Mary Nelson,
November 27, 1747

McConchie, William. Married Bridget Whitecotton,
November 10, 1747

Million, William Bennet. Son of Robert and Grace,
born December 23, 1747

MacMurry, Ann. Married John Donaldson,
December 31, 1747

MacCarthy, Elizabeth.   Married Simson Bailey,
December 24, 1747
MacMachon, Byron.   Married Jane Moore,
December 30, 1747
Moore, Jane.   Married Byron MacMachon,
December 30, 1747
Macaboy, Mortbrough.   Married Elizabeth Pumphrey,
December 27, 1747
More, Mary.   Daughter of Nathaniel and Sarah, born
Jnauary 31, 1748
Million, William Bennet.   Baptized
September 22, 1748
Merringham, Jane.   Married Thomas Bettson,
April 14, 1748
McCarty, Eleanor.   Married John Summon,
April 10, 1748
Mitchell, Barnaby Le Gosh.   Son of Jedidiah and
Lydia, born March 10, 1748
Murray, Phobe.   Daughter ot Anthony, born
April 1, 1748
Manzy, Peter.   Son of Peter and Elizabeth, born
May 19, 1738
McConchie, Richard.   Son of William, born
July 10, 1748
Minor, Susannah.   Daughter of William, born
August 22, 1748

Moncure, Ann.   Daughter of Rev. John Moncure and
                Frances, his wife, born October 17, 1748
Moring, James.   Died at Capt. William Mountjoy's,
                                September 23, 1748
Mountjoy, George.   Son of William and Phillis, born
                                September 9, 1748
Martin, Lacy.   Married James Green, October 4, 1748
Mason, William.   Son of John and Mary, born
                                November 30, 1748
Murphy, Peter.   Was baptized November 8, 1748
Monroe, Thomas.   Was baptized November 2, 1748
Mitchel, Samuel.   Married Bridget Berry,
                                January 30, 1749
Montgomery, John.   Son of John, born
                                April 3, 1749
Minor, Amelia.   Daughter of John, born July 7, 1749
Morris, James.   Died at John Smith's,
                                August 28, 1749
Million, Robert.   Married Heziah Holliday,
                                December 14, 1749
McCoy, Alexander.   Son of Mundy and John, born
                                October 20, 1749
Million, John.   Son of Robert, died October 1, 1749
Montgomery, John.   Son of John, died
                                October 22, 1749
Macaboy, Murthough.   Died January 1, 1750

Macaboy, Murthough. Son of Murthough and
Elizabeth, born January 19, 1750
Moss, Meredith. Son of Silvester and Elizabeth, born
January 4, 1750
Mitchell, William. Son of Samuel and Bridget, born
January 27, 1750
Matheny, Mary. Departed this life, January 12, 1750
More, Sarah. Daughter of Sarah and Nathaniel, born
April 26, 1750
More, Sarah. Died at William George's plantation,
March 5, 1750
Matheny, Job. Son of William and Ann, born
February 6, 1750
Millian, Benjamin. Son of Robert, born July 5, 1750
Macconchie, Bridget. Married Stephen Pilcher,
December 1, 1750
Montgomery, Robert. Son of John and Mary, born
November 13, 1750
Murray, Margaret. Married John Ogiboy,
October 7, 1750
Murray, Anthony. Departed this life at his own
home, October 5, 1750
Mings, James. Married Susannah Pattison,
September 7, 1750
Mathews, George. Married ——— Chinn,
August 15, 1750

Murdock, John. Married Margaret Strother,
                                    October 26, 1750
Million, Jemima. Daughter of Robert, born
                                    November 13, 1750
Mobley, Elizabeth. Died at Henry Robinson's,
                                    September 4, 1750
Minor, John, Sr. Died at his home,
                                    January 12, 1750-1
Mason, John. Son of John and Mary, born
                                    February 18, 1750
Morris, Young. Son of Griffin, born March 25, 1751
Mason, Mary Thomas. Married Samuel Selden,
                                    April 11, 1751
Mathews, Mary. Married John Waller, July 4, 1751
Marony, Mary. Married Solomon Carter,
                                    May 26, 1751
Montjoy, Elizabeth. Daughter of William and
                                    Phillis, born May 26, 1751
Matheny, James. Married Lizzie Gain,
                                    December 12, 1751
MacCollough, Benjamin. Married Elizabeth Whitson,
                                    December 19, 1751
MacCothough, Hannah. Married Benjamin Tolson,
                                    December 31, 1751
Manatear, Alexander. Married Merriam Belsher,
                                    December 24, 1751

Maccullough, Mary.   Married Thomas Ashby,
                        November 14, 1751
More, William.   Married Mary Green,
                        November 28, 1751
Monroe, Isabel.   Daughter of Thomas and Catharine,
                        born November 12, 1751
Monslow, John.   Died at the house of John Water's,
                        October 3, 1751
McDaniel, Margaret.   Daughter of Jane and James,
                        born January 8, 1752
Mitchel, Elizabeth.   Daughter of Samuel and Bridget,
                        born January 19, 1752
Mays, James.   Son of Joseph, was born
                        February 1, 1752
MacDaniel, Margaret.   Married John Powell,
                        February 10, 1752
Manzy, Elizabeth.   Married Peter Murphy,
                        February 9, 1752
Murphy, Peter.   Married Elizabeth Manzy,
                        February 9, 1752
MacCollough, Joseph.   Married Martha King,
                        February 9, 1752
Mays, William.   Married Sarah Laythium,
                        February 9, 1752
Montgomery, Elizabeth.   Daughter of John and
                        Mary, born April 20, 1752

Mathews, Jean. Daughter of John, born
June 23, 1752

Moss, Triplet. Son of Sylvester and Elizabeth, born
August 9, 1752

Mills, Elizabeth. Married Edward West,
October 6, 1752

McCoy, William. Son of Mudy and Ann, born
October 15, 1752

More, John. Son of Nathaniel and Sarah, born
September 20, 1752

Murphy, Eleanor. Daughter of Peter and Elizabeth,
baptized October 29, 1752

Macinteer, William. Son of Alexander, born
November 7, 1752

Mays, George. Son of William and Sarah, born
February 7, 1753

Mason, Daniel. Married Elizabeth Nelson,
January 30, 1753

Matheny, Mary. Daughter of James and Elizabeth,
born January 16, 1753

Moore, Isaac. Son of William and Mary, born
March 25, 1753

Matheny, Mary. Daughter of William and Ann,
born April 2, 1753

Matheny, Mary. Married Moses Grisby,
August 26, 1753

Moncure, Jean.   Daughter of the Rev. John Moncure,
born May 22, 1753

Matheny, William.   Son of Thomas and Hannah,
born July 26, 1753

Mason, Nelson.   Son of John and Mary, born
August 6, 1753

Million, Sithy.   Daughter of Robert of Keziah, born
April 2, 1753

Montjoy, Margaret.   Daughter of William and Phillis,
born April 2, 1753

Mills, Margaret.   Married James Sconkraft,
October 14, 1753

Mays, George.   Son of William, died
November 14, 1753

Mays, Lydia.   Daughter of Joseph and Sarah, born
February 25, 1754

Montgomery, John.   Son of John and Mary, born
January 26, 1754

Manzeys, George.   Departed this life at John
Manzey's, January 10, 1754

Macculough, William.   Son of Benjamin and
Elizabeth, born May 19, 1754

Macinteer, Gabriel.   Son of Alexander, born
May 24, 1754

More, Ann.   Daughter of Nathaniel and Sarah, born
June 8, 1754

Mays, Jeany. Daughter of William and Sarah, born
October 15, 1754

More, William. Son of William and Mary, born
December 30, 1754

Murphy, Ann. Daughter of Peter and Elizabeth,
born February 14, 1755

Montjoy, Margaret. Daughter of Capt. William
Montjoy, died March 1, 1755

Matheny, Ann. Daughter of Ann and William, born
March 18, 1755

Morris, Anthony. Son of Griffin and Elizabeth, born
January 28, 1755

McCarty, Ignatius. Departed this life at his home,
February 18, 1755

McCarty, Frances. Married John Diskin,
June 19, 1755

Macquatty, David. Married Mary Skaines,
May 6, 1755

Macquatty, Nancy. Daughter of David and Mary,
born July 10, 1755

Maccoy, Elizabeth. Daughter of Murdy, died
June 5, 1755

Mason, Sarah. Daughter of Daniel and Elizabeth,
born December 15, 1755

MacDaniel, Reuben. Son of James and Jean, born
November 22, 1755

Maccaboy, Elizabeth.   Married James Givin,
>> October 5, 1755

MacCarty, Margaret.   Married Stephen Hansford,
>> October 14, 1755

Mason, George.   Married Elizabeth Durrest,
>> October 21, 1755

Maccullough, Sarah.   Married John Ashby,
>> February 26, 1756

Murphy, Isaac.   Married Catharine Ashby,
>> January 1, 1756

Million, Sarah Ann.   Daughter of Robert and Keziah,
>> born February 13, 1756

Mays, Joseph.   Son of Joseph and Sarah, born
>> April 18, 1756

Manuel, ———.   Died at James Phillips,
>> September 10, 1753

Martyor, Margaret.   Married John Lunsford,
>> June 6, 1756

More, Jane.   Daughter of Nathaniel, born
>> June 17, 1756

Mananteer, Elijah.   Son of Alexander, born
>> June 14, 1756

Montjoy, George.   Son of William and Phillis, died
>> June 1, 1756

Mays, Robert.   Married Elizabeth Bolling,
>> December 27, 1756

Moore, Elizabeth. Daughter of William, born
December 23, 1756
Murphy, Lydia. Daughter of Isaac and Catharine,
born November 15, 1756
Monroe, John. Married Sarah Harrison,
September 23, 1756
Matheny, James. Son of James and Elizabeth, born
September 9, 1756
Maccullough, James. Son of Benjamin and Elizabeth,
born November 29, 1756
Mason, Lewis. Son of John, born February 5, 1757
Mason, Frances. Daughter of George, born
January 16, 1757
Mathews, Mary. Married James Turner,
March 3, 1757
Martin, Sarah. Married Moses Fletcher,
July 10, 1757
McCoy, Feanly. Married Jane Thomas, July 18, 1757
McCoy, Daniel. Son of Feanly, born
October 10, 1757
Mays, Benjamin. Son of William and Elizabeth,
born September 10, 1757
Mountjoy, George. Son of William and Phillis, born
September 1, 1757
Mays, George. Son of Joseph and Sarah, born
January 1, 1758

Macinteer, Rodah. Was baptized April 9, 1758

Millian, Jeany. Daughter of Robert and Keziah, born
April 19, 1758

Moncure, Frances, Jr. Married Travers, Daniel, at
"Claremont," October 7, 1762, by the
Rev. Mr. James Scott

Moncure, William. Son of John and Ann, born
September 21, 1774

Matheny, William. Married Ann Sims,
September 10, 1747

Moses, Mary. Married Andrew Watson,
September 26, 1742

Monslow, John. Married Jean Waters,
October 26, 1748

N.

Norton, Elizabeth. Married Charles Colson,
February 1, 1739

Nelson, Margaret. Daughter of Alexander and
Margaret, born January 14, 1739

Nelson, Lettie. Daughter of Henry and Sarah, born
March 10, 1740

Nelson, Lettie. Daughter of Alexander, died
September 28, 1740

Nelson, Hannah. Daughter of John and Mary, born
October 19, 1740

Normand, James. Son of Thomas, born
September 13, 1740
Nelson, John. Married Mary Toby,
February 10, 1740
Normand, William. Son of Thomas and Martha,
born November 11, 1741
Nelson, Henry. Married Jean Goodwin,
October 18, 1742
Normand, George. Son of Thomas and Elizabeth,
born June 25, 1743
Nubal, Priscilla. Daughter of Samuel and Hannah,
born June 21, 1743
Nelson, William. Son of Henry and Jean, born
August 14, 1743
Nelson, Susannah. Daughter of Henry and Sarah,
born October 25, 1743
Nickolas, Elee. Married Nathaniel More,
December 31, 1743
Northcutt, Elizabeth. Married Anthony Philips,
December 26, 1743
Northcutt, Martha. Daughter of William and
Margery, born August 10, 1744
Nelson, Alexander. Married Margaret Butler,
February 21, 1745
Nelson, Henry. Son of Henry and Jean, born
August 2, 1745

Nelson, John.   Married Sarah Whitson,
>> December 7, 1745

Newbold, William.   Son of Samuel and Joannah,
>> born December 12, 1745

Nelson, Alexander.   Departed this life,
>> October 19, 1745

Nelson, William.   Son of Alexander, born
>> February 2, 1746

Normand, Thomas.   Son of Thomas and Elizabeth,
>> born August 10, 1746

Nelson, Lydia.   Daughter of John and Sarah, born
>> September 24, 1746

Noble, Joshua.   Married Hannah Blackman,
>> September 7, 1746

Nelson, Frances.   Daughter of Henry and Sarah, born
>> January 15, 1747

Nelson, Jemima.   Daughter of Henry and Jane, born
>> January, 28, 1747

Nelson, John.   Was born July 10, 1747

Nelson, Mary.   Married John Mason,
>> November 27, 1747

Nowland, Richard.   Married Jane Wright,
>> December 20, 1747

Nelson, Elizabeth,   Was born October 9, 1747

Nelson, Margaret.   Married John Powwell,
>> September 4, 1748

Nelson, John.   Died at John Powwail's,

October 14, 1748

Nelson, Nanny.   Daughter of John and Sarah, born

January 11, 1749

Nelson, Alexander.   Son of Alexander and Mary,

born March 30, 1749

Nelson, Henry.   Departed this life, February 29, 1749

Normand, Ann.   Daughter of Thomas, born

February 14, 1750

Northcutt, Mary.   Married Haswel Hardwick,

December 25, 1750

Nunn, Thomas.   Son of John, born January 1, 1750–1

Nelson, Mary.   Daughter of John and Sarah, born

March 2, 1751

Nelson, John.   Son of Alexander, born March 5, 1751

Nelson, John.   Son of Henry and Jane, born

May 21, 1751

Northcutt, Sarah.   Married John Foxworthy,

December 25, 1751

Nubal, Sarah.   Married Thomas Foxworthy,

September 29, 1751

Nicolas, John.   Married Mary Hyden, April 23, 1752

Nickolas, John.   Son of John, born

November 7, 1752

Nelson, Elizabeth.   Married Daniel Mason,

January 30, 1753

Nelson, Margaret.   Daughter of Alexander and
                                Margaret, born January 10, 1753
Nickson, Patty.   Daughter of John and Rachel, born
                                        October 2, 1754
Nowland, Jean.   Married John Brown,
                                        August 24, 1755
Nelson, George.   Son of Alexander and Margaret,
                                born December 4, 1755
Nelson, Jesse.   Son of John and Sarah, born
                                        January 22, 1756
Noble, Joshua.   Son of Joshua and Hannah, born
                                        August 17, 1756
Noble, Jean.   Married Derby Driscal,
                                        October 4, 1756
Noxal, Saxfield.   Married Ann Boning,
                                        August 1, 1757
Nelson, Jean.   Daughter of John, born
                                        January 24, 1758
Nelson, Alexander.   Departed this life,
                                        June 20, 1758

O.

Onsby, Elizabeth.   Married Carty Wells,
                                        September 10, 1738
O'Cane, John.   The son of Derby and Susanna, born
                                        March 20, 1739

O'Neal, Timothy. Married Elizabeth Mathews,
April 22, 1739
O'Cane, Derby. Married Susannah Smith,
December 16, 1739
O'Cane, Thomas. Son of Derby, born May 4, 1740
O'Daneal, Priscilla. Daughter of Timothy and
Elizabeth, born April 1, 1743
O'Cane, Mary. Daughter of Susannah and Derby,
born May 9, 1745
Oram, Rachel. Married John Hart, March 23, 1746
O'Daneal, Elizabeth. Married William Thornberry,
July 10, 1746
O'Cain, James. Son of Derby and Susannah, born
October 4, 1747
Ogiloy, John. Married Margaret Murray,
October 7, 1750
Ogiloy, Ann. Daughter of John, born April 27, 1750
O'Cain, Daniel. Son of Derby and Susannah, born
April 1, 1750
Osbon, Judith. Daughter of William, born
February 2, 1751
O'Cain, Derby. Son of Derby, born March 4, 1753
Ogiloy, Winifred. Daughter of John, born
July 18, 1751
Ogiloy, Margaret. Daughter of Margaret and John,
born April 3, 1754

O'Banion, Ann.   Married Alexander Farrow,
                                    October 5, 1753
Owendownney, John.   Died at Priscilla Hays',
                                    January 22, 1754
Oliver, Keziah.   Daughter of John and Mary, born
                                    April 5, 1754
O'Cain, Henry.   Son of Derby and Susannah, born
                                    August 4, 1755
O'Daneal, James.   Married Theodsian Congers,
                                    October 19, 1755
O'Daneal, William Scott.   Son of James and
                    Theodsian, born August 10, 1756

P.

Powel, John.   Son of Charles and Elizabeth, born
                                    September 20, 1731
Powel, Peter.   Son of Charles and Elizabeth, born
                                    February 17, 1733
Powell, Elizabeth.   Daughter of Charles and
                    Elizabeth, born April 26, 1735
Powel, Martha.   Daughter of Charles and Elizabeth
                    born September 26, 1736
Pettigrew, James.   Son of John and Mary, born
                                    April 2, 1737
Pepper, Mary.   Married James Suddeth,
                                    May 13, 1738

Parker, Martha.   Married Peter Bailen,

> August 6, 1738

Pritchet, Philip's wife, Elizabeth, died

> January 29, 1739

Peddicoat, Jannet.   Married Moses Rowley,

> May 16, 1739

Prim, John.   Married Margaret Welch,

> September 9, 1739

Peddicoat, John.   Son of John and Mary, born

> December 28, 1739

Powton, Edward.   Married Mary Matheney,

> November 20, 1739

Pattin, William.   Married Joyie Mcinteer,

> January 27, 1740

Porter, Thomas.   Departed this life,

> February 26, 1740

Payton, Catharine.   Married William Scrogging,

> February 18, 1740

Powel, Charles.   Son of Charles and Elizabeth, born

> May 26, 1740

Prim, William.   Son of John and Margaret, born

> July 28, 1740

Payton, Alexander.   Married Jane Heffermon,

> May 20, 1740

Phips, Stephen.   Married Rosamond Mayow,

> June 1, 1740

Paddeth, Thomas.   Son of James and Elizabeth, died
February 8, 1741

Patten, Margaret.   Daughter of William and Joyie,
born March 10, 1741

Peyton, Elizabeth.   Daughter of John and Eleanor,
born July 1, 1741

Perry, Mary.   Daughter of Prudence, born
July 21, 1741

Philips, James.   Married Elizabeth Griffin,
September 27, 1741

Philips, Lettie.   Daughter of James and Elizabeth,
born November 22, 1741

Punton, Edward.   Departed this life, January 22, 1741

Payton, William.   Son of John, born July 25, 1742

Pritchet, William.   Married Jane Cook,
January 26, 1742

Pritchet, Philip.   Married Catharine Cole,
January 24, 1742

Pritchet, Anne.   Daughter of Philip and Catharine,
born September 4, 1742

Pattin, Jean.   Daughter of William and Jean, born
December 23, 1742

Peyton, Henry.   Son of John and Eleanor, born
March 9, 1743

Pike, Margary.   Died at Michael Pike's,
February 27, 1744

Payton, Rachel   Daughter of John and Worth, born
August 22, 1743

Philips, Anthony.   Married Elizabeth Northcutt,
December 26, 1743

Pritchet, Catharine.   Daughter of Philip, born
December 28, 1743

Powel, Peggy.   Daughter of Charles and Betty, born
April 8, 1744

Powel, Charles,   Departed this life, April 30, 1744

Pritchet, Lewis.   Married Mary Littimore,
March 31, 1744

Poole, Sarah.   Married John Foley, December 11, 1744

Philips, William.   Son of James and Elizabeth, born
November 1, 1744

Pritchet, Philip, Sr.   Departed this life,
November 14, 1744

Pownall, Elizabeth.   Married John Cooper,
March 30, 1745

Powtone, Isabel.   Daughter of Mary, born
February 9, 1745

Philips, Dorcas.   Daughter of Anthony and Elizabeth,
born March 10, 1745

Philips, William.   Son of John and Mary, born
February 2, 1745

Perender, Eleanor.   Married Thomas Massey,
June 26, 1745

Parson, Sarah.   Daughter of Anne and William, born
May 26, 1745
Powell, Elizabeth.   Married Duke Whalbone,
December 3, 1745
Plummer, Mary.   Married Richard Matthis,
October 5, 1745
Philips, Mary.   Daughter of Robert and Elizabeth,
died October 16, 1745
Page, Sarah.   Married Nathaniel More,
September 11, 1745
Porter, Howsen.   Married John Stark,
January 1, 1746
Powel, Richard.   Son of Mary, born
February 14, 1746
Prim, Anne.   Daughter of John and Margaret, born
September 15, 1746
Payton, Charles.   Son of John and Werth, born
November 1, 1746
Proctor, Edward.   Married Anny Weeks,
February 15, 1747
Porch, Robert.   Departed this life April 5, 1747
Peyton, Anne.   Married Thomas Harrison,
July 2, 1747
Peyton, Eleanor.   Wife of John, died October 5, 1747
Pumphrey, Elizabeth.   Married Morthough McCaboy,
December 27, 1747

Patten, Ann. Daughter of William, born
>> December 23, 1747
Phillips, Mary. Daughter of James Philips, born
>> January 15, 1748
Patten, Ann. Daughter of William, died
>> January 11, 1748
Pritchett, Lewis. Son of Lewis and Mary, born
>> February 17, 1748
Powell, Renn. Son of Mary, born February 2, 1748
Pane, Francis. Son of Francis, born March 18, 1748
Pane, Francis. Son of Francis, died April 15, 1748
Patterson, John. Was born May 8, 1748
Peyton, Elizabeth. Daughter of John, died
>> May 11, 1748
Pully, Robert. Married Mary Thomson,
>> August 28, 1748
Price, William. Married Sarah Allenthrop,
>> August 8, 1748
Petter, John. Married Judith Lunsford,
>> February 27, 1748
Pearson, Hannah. Departed this life,
>> November 12, 1748
Porch, Thomas. Married Rachel Limbrick,
>> July 22, 1748
Punell, Emmeal. Son of Richard and Mary,
>> July 20, 1748

Peyton, Philip.   Married Winifred Bussel,
September 15, 1748
Pownall, John.   Married Margaret Nelson,
September 4, 1748
Pilcher, Stephen.   Married Lucy Clarke,
November 7, 1748
Parsons, Ann.   Departed this life,
November 26, 1748
Pownall, Margaret.   Daughter of John, born
November 10, 1748
Peyton, Valentine.   Son of Philip and Winifred, born
March 19, 1749
Pattison, Sarah, alias Congers.   Married Thomas
Hampton, January 1, 1749
Pannel, Mary.   Died at William Patton's,
October 25, 1749
Porter, Calvert.   Married Elizabeth Cash,
Sepember 21, 1749
Porter, Joseph.   Son of Calvert and Elizabeth, born
October 21, 1749
Patton, Sarah.   Daughter of William, born
November 24, 1749
Pilcher, Samuel.   Son of Stephen and Elizabeth, born
January 5, 1750
Pilcher, Elizabeth.   Departed this life,
January 23, 1750

Pilcher, James. Son of Stephen, born

> February 17, 1750

Payne, Edward. Married Ann Holland Congers,

> February 27, 1750

Paterson, Behethelan. Daughter of Mary, born

> April 17, 1750

Pyke, Ann. Married Henry Hurst,

> March 20, 1750

Peyton, Jeremiah. Son of John and Werth, born

> January 29, 1750

Prim, John. Son of John and Margaret, born

> May 17, 1750

Pilcher, Stephen. Married Bridget MacConchie,

> December 1, 1750

Powell, Mary. Died at William Hendale's,

> November 21, 1750

Pattison, Susannah. Married James Mings,

> September 7, 1750

Phillips, Dianah. Daughter of Anthony and
Elizabeth, born February 22, 1751

Pattison, Lydia Alvin. Daughter of Elizabeth, born

> May 4, 1751

Payton, Nancy. Daughter of John and Werth, born

> November 13, 1751

Peyton, John. Married Elizabeth Waller,

> November 17, 1751

Prim, Thomas.   Son of John and Margaret, born
December 13, 1751
Porter, Calvert.   Son of Calvert and Elizabeth, born
March 1, 1752
Powel, John.   Married Margaret MacDaniel,
February 10, 1752
Phillips, Dianah.   Departed this life,
February 20, 1752
Porch, Rachel.   Married William Burton,
October 7, 1753
Powel, Jemima.   Daughter of John and Margaret,
born November 9, 1753
Petter, Jane.   Daughter of John and Judith, born
December 11, 1753
Porch, Ann.   Married William Berry, February 26, 1754
Porter, Thomas.   Son of Calvert and Elizabeth, born
January 11, 1754
Peirson, Nanny.   Daughter of William and Sarah,
born January 18, 1754
Pilcher, Mary.   Died at Alexander Macanteer's,
January 25, 1754
Porter, John.   Departed this life, July 14, 1754
Parinder, Elizabeth.   Married William Adie,
July 25, 1754
Peyton, John Rousey.   Son of John, baptized
November 17, 1754

Peyton, Dr. Valentine. Departed this life,

November 28, 1754

Patten, John and William. Sons of William and

Joyie, born December 28, 1754

Powell, Patty. Daughter of John and Margaret, born

November 17, 1755

Patterson, Ruth. Daughter of Mary, born

September 19, 1755

Porter, Frances. Daughter of Calvert and Elizabeth,

born January 12, 1756

Porter, Thomas. Was baptized February 23, 1756

Powell, Martha. Married John Goldsmith,

January 19, 1756

Porter, Joseph. Married Jemima Smith,

February 24, 1756

Patten, William. Married Isabella Kennedy,

December 19, 1756

Philips, Lettie. Married John Cummings,

February 21, 1757

Porter Charity. Daughter of Calvert and Elizabeth,

born Septenber 9, 1757

Pilford, Elizabeth. Married William Cooper,

January 5, 1758

Peyton, John. Married Susannnah Lunsford,

March 28, 1758

Q.

Quidley, Stephen.   Son of William, died

February 8, 1745

R.

Robison, Philip.   Married Margaret Spoldin,

November 26, 1738

Ross, Rebecca.   Daughter of William and Margaret,

born February 28, 1739

Rowley, Moses.   Married Jannet Peddicoat,

May 16, 1739

Rout, Hannah.   Daughter of Peter and Martha, born

January 31, 1740

Renny, John.   Married Mary Linton, April 6, 1740

Richards, John.   Married Mary Latham,

January 24, 1740

Renny, Jeremiah.   Son of John and Mary, born

November 18, 1740

Robinson, John.   Son of Benjamin and Catharine,

born December 22, 1740

Reddish, Jean.   Daughter of Robert, born

January 8, 1741

Robinson, Mary.   Daughter of Christopher and

Eleanor, born January 1, 1741

Robinson, Sarah.   Married John Kirke,

June 23, 1741

Richards, Francis. Son of John and Mary, born
                                May 25, 1741
Renny, Jacob. Son of William and Barbara, born
                                August 27, 1741
Raper, Susanna. Daughter of Thomas and Elizabeth,
                        born September 30, 1741
Rogers, William. Son of Rachel, born
                                June 1, 1742
Rogers, William. Son of Richard and Mary, born
                                October 13, 1741
Ross, John. Son of William and Margaret, born
                                June 4, 1742
Routt, John. Son of Peter and Martha, born
                                December 13, 1742
Renny, Prisly. Son of John and Mary, born
                                December 28, 1742
Rassan, William. Married Priscilla Manzey,
                                October 27, 1743
Robinson, Nanny. Daughter of Benjamin and
                        Catharine, born April 23, 1743
Reaves, George. Married Anne Webster,
                                April 3, 1743
Robinson, Ann. Married William Green,
                                December 18, 1743
Robinson, Christopher. Son of Christopher and
                        Eleanor, born February 25, 1744

Rush, Benjamin.   Married Alice Grigsby,
                                    April 1, 1744
Ross, John.   Son of William and Margaret, died
                                    September 4, 1744
Rice, Lydia.   Daughter of John and Ann, born
                                    November 9, 1744
Raper, Elizabeth.   Daughter of Frances, died
                                    October 12, 1744
Richards, Francis.   Son of John, died
                                    November 8, 1744
Renny, Tabitha.   Daughter of John and Mary, born
                                    March 8, 1745
Routt, James.   Son of Peter and Martha, born
                                    July 29, 1745
Ryley, Thomas.   Son of John and Elizabeth, born
                                    July 12, 1745
Reynolds, Peter.   Married Easter Carr, June 2, 1745
Rhodes, Mary.   Married Isaac Basriet,
                                    May 18, 1745
Ryan, William.   Son of Michael and Winefred, died
                                    December 4, 1745
Robinson, Christopher, Jr.   Died December 8, 1745
Ransdell, Elizabeth.   Daughter of Wharton and
                                    Margaret, born April 6, 1746
Regnold, James.   Married Margaret Deckon,
                                    August 19, 1746

Rhodes, Sanford. Son of John and Martha, born
December 13, 1746
Robinson, William. Son of Christopher and Eleanor,
born November 3, 1746
Rosser, Sarah. Married Hayward Todd,
September 7, 1746
Robinson, Rebecca. Married William Godfrey,
October 26, 1746
Radcliffe, Eleanor. Married Thomas Turner,
September 13, 1746
Rayle, Hugh. Son of John, born February 24, 1747
Richetts, Sarah Ann. Daughter of Thomas, born
September 21, 1747
Raper, John. Son of Elizabeth, born June 26, 1747
Renny, Calab. Son of John and Mary, born
May 20, 1747
Ryan, Daniel. Son of Michael and Winifred, born
September 2, 1747
Robertson, John. Married Rose Jones,
October 15, 1747
Robe, Isabel. Married Thomas Weddell,
January 3, 1748
Read, Mary. Daughter of Robert and Dorothy, born
January 5, 1748
Rhodes, Martha. The wife of John, died
April 7, 1748

Ryan, Daniel. Son of Michael and Winifred, died
                                          March 7, 1748
Read, Mary. Was baptized March 13, 1748
Robinson, Mary. The wife of Henry, died
                                          March 26, 1748
Ramsdell, Edward. Son of Wharton, born
                                          June 19, 1748
Read, John. Married Ann Sebastian, July 21, 1748
Rhodes, John. Departed this life, November 12, 1748
Robinson, Elizabeth. Married John Rabbing,
                                          December 29, 1748
Rabbing, John. Married Elizabeth Robinson,
                                          December 29, 1748
Robinson, Sarah. Married James Fernsley,
                                          November 3, 1748
Robinson, Josham. Married John Sprayburry,
                                          November 9, 1748
Robinson, James. Son of Christopher and Eleanor,
                                          born April 16, 1749
Ryley, John. Son of John and Elizabeth, born
                                          March 4, 1749
Rabbing, John. Died at William Kinz's,
                                          February 4, 1749
Routt, Betty. Daughter of Peter, died June 27, 1749
Renny, Lydia. Daughter of John and Mary, born
                                          July 30, 1749

Rice, John. Departed this life, September 2, 1749

Reiliegh, Ann. Departed this life,

September 24, 1749

Robinson, Benjamin. Married Sarah Stacy,

January 2, 1750

Redman, Ann. Daughter of Patrick, born

December 7, 1749

Robinson, Nathaniel. Son of Benjamin and Sarah,

born April 22, 1750

Ransdell, Wharton. Son of Wharton and Margaret,

born January 12, 1750

Robinson, Henry. Married Winifred Bailis,

August 1, 1750

Ross, William. Son of William and Margaret, born

September 11, 1750

Risen, John. Married Hannah Chinn,

October 20, 1750

Ryley, Charles. Son of John and Elizabeth, born

October 11, 1750

Reeds, Elizabeth. Married William Spilman,

February, 25, 1751

Runnils, Frank. Died March 1C, 1751

Renny, Butler. Son of John and Mary, born

April 18, 1751

Redman, Sarah. Daughter of Patrick, born

April 16, 1752

Riley, Nanny.   Daughter of Nickolas, born
April 17, 1752

Rhodes, Ann.   Married Robert Fristoe,
February 23, 1752

Robinson, Carty.   Daughter of Benjamin and Sarah,
born January 8, 1752

Rankins, Ann.   Daughter of George and Sarah, born
January 14, 1752

Rounde, David.   Married Mary Turner,
January 28, 1753

Ryley, George.   Son of John and Elizabeth, born
February 28, 1753

Rose, ·William.   Married Sarah Grigsby,
June 5, 1753

Renny, John.   Son of John and Mary, born
November 8, 1753

Raleigh, Henry.   Son of Nickolas and Winifred, born
November 21, 1753

Ryley, George.   Son of John and Elizabeth, died
October 5, 1753

Routt, William.   Married Winifred Byram,
November 27, 1753

Riding, Thomas.   Son of James and Mary, born
April 27, 1753

Read, John.   Married Margaret Allenthrop,
March 5, 1754

Randal, Catharine. Married George Bussel,
January 8, 1754
Robinson, George. Son of Sarah and Benjamin, born
February 7, 1754
Redman, John. Son of Patrick and Elizabeth, born
July 18, 1754
Routt, Peter. Son of William and Winifred, born
October 22, 1754
Richards, John. Married Susannah Thomas Heath,
March 6, 1754
Richetts, Sarah Ann. Daughter of Thomas and
Sarah, baptized January 26, 1755
Riggins, Bridget. Married John Flitter,
March 16, 1755
Robinson, Simon. Married Mary Jack,
August 3, 1755
Robinson, Benjamin. Married Elizabeth Stacey,
May 25, 1755
Roach, Thomas. Married Ann Cooke,
December 28, 1755
Richards, Elizabeth. Was baptized
January 26, 1756
Ryley, James. Son of Nickolas and Winifred, born
January 21, 1756
Robinson, Lishea. Daughter of Benjamin and Sarah,
born February 25, 1756

Routt, William. Son of William and Winifred, born
May 29, 1756

Rigg, Lewis. Son of John and Betty, born
March 17, 1757

Rowels, Jesse. Son of Henry and Isabell, born
January 28, 1757

Renny, Sennot. Son of John and Mary, born
February 25, 1757

Ryley, Betty. Daughter of Nickolas and Winifred,
born March 20, 1757

Reiley, Mary. Daughter of John and Elizabeth, born
March 20, 1757

Raper, Elizabeth. Married Alexander Sutor,
May 8, 1757

Ryan, Michael. Departed this life,
October 10, 1757

Ross, William. Departed this life, December 26, 1757

Rose, William. Married Jane Grigsby,
March 14, 1758

Robinson, Benjamin. Son of Benjamin and Sarah,
born June 21, 1758

Riddle, Thomas. Married Bridget Amely,
February 5, 1758

Roath, Patrick. Married Elizabeth Wise,
October 9, 1742

S.

Stark, Sarah. Daughter of James and Elizabeth, born
August 23, 1731

Stark, Jean. Daughter of James and Elizabeth, born
February 1, 1733

Stark, Anne. Daughter of James and Elizabeth, born
February 9, 1736

Stark, Benjamin. Son of James and Elizabeth, born
September 27, 1738

Suddeth, James. Married Mary Pepper, May 13, 1738

Strother, Elizabeth. Married John Frogg,
November 9, 1738

Spoldin, Margaret. Married Philip Robinson,
November 26, 1738

Smith, Elizabeth. Married Charles Cornish,
December 17, 1738

Simpson, Mary. Departed this life,
January 15, 1739

Scott, Helen. Daughter of James and Sarah, born
June 7, 1739

Smith, Susannah. Married Derby O'Cain,
December 16, 1739

Stuart, William. Son of James and Mary, born
January 1, 1740

Scogging, William. Married Catharine Payton,
February 18, 1740

Stuart, James.   Married Mary Dunaway,
                                    February 12, 1740
Simpson, Million.   Daughter ot William and Diana,
                                    born May 5, 1740
Strong, John.   Son of Nathaniel and Mary, born
                                    June 22, 1740
Smith, Withers and George.   Sons of Nathaniel and
                          Elizabeth, born June 13, 1740
Sinclair, George.   Son of George and Winifred, born
                                    November 7, 1740
Scott, Alexander.   Son of James and Sarah, born
                                    July 10, 1740
Simpson, John.   Married Silent Johnston,
                                    August 17, 1740
Smith, William.   Son of Henry and Sarah, died
                                    September 17, 1740
Sinclair, George.   Departed this life,
                                    January 12, 1741
Sinclair, Margaret.   Married Francis Tennel,
                                    November 9, 1740
Scott, Sarah.   Daughter of Rev. James Scott, born
                                    January 22, 1741
Smith, Henry.   Son of Henry and Sarah, born
                                    February 3, 1741
Stacey, Simon.   Married Judith Tolson,
                                    August 22, 1741

Stanly, Marjory. Married Edmond Webster,
                              November 20, 1741
Short, Jean. The wife of John, died
                              December 9, 1741
Sturdy, Margaret. Married Parish Garner,
                              January 21, 1741
Scott, James. Son of Rev. James and Sarah, born
                              January 8, 1742
Smith, Mary. Married William Cammel,
                              July 25, 1742
Stacey, Sarah. Daughter of Judith and Simon, born
                              August 20, 1742
Stuart, James. Son of Mary and James, born
                              October 26, 1742
Sinclair, Winifred. Daughter of George and
                      Winifred, born October 3, 1742
Stuart, William. Died at Mr. Scott's,
                              October 22, 1742
Sinclair, Winifred. Wife of George, died
                              October 22, 1742
Spinks, Enoch. Son of John and Rosamond, born
                              November 10, 1742
Smith, William. Son of Henry and Sarah, born
                              October 28, 1742
Sturdy, Elizabeth. Daughter of Robert and
                      Elizabeth died November 20, 1742

Smith, Temple. Son of Nathaniel, died
                                    January 24, 1743
Smith, Susannah. Married John Cotton,
                                    February 17, 1743
Simmonds, Jemima. Daughter of George and
                            Elizabeth, born March 17, 1743
Stacey, Katharine. Daughter of Elizabeth, born
                                    March 17, 1743
Smith, Anne. Daughter of Robert and Phillis, born
                                    May 21, 1743
Simpson, Alexander. Married Catharine Fant,
                                    July 17, 1743
Sinclair, Clementina. Daughter of George, died
                                    July 21, 1743
Stungfellow, Benjamin. Married Mary Foley,
                                    June 15, 1743
Shaw, John. Married Mary Waters,
                                    June 12, 1743
Simpson, Elizabeth. Married John Whitcomb,
                                    November 24, 1743
Spoldin, Francis. Son of Thomas and Elizabeth,
                                    born January 7, 1743
Smith, Mary. Married John Montgomery,
                                    January 16, 1744
Strother, Margaret. Married George Molton,
                                    April 6, 1744

Stacey, Benjamin. Son of Simon and Judith, born
                                    April 7, 1744
Suthard, Rose. Married Silent Jeffreys,
                                    January 19, 1744
Suddeth, Mary. Married Edward Boling, May 4, 1744
Shorter, Anne. Married Francis Tyler, May 17, 1744
Sinclair, Patience. Married William Young,
                                    July 23, 1744
Stark, Daniel. Son of James and Elizabeth, born
                                    May 30, 1744
Simpson, Priscilla. Daughter of George and
                        Margaret, born September 26, 1744
Savage, Eleanor. Married John Hogg,
                                    December 19, 1744
Smith, Temple. Son of Nathaniel, born
                                    April 26, 1745
Suddeth, Lawrence. Married Dorothy West,
                                    April 18, 1745
Scott, Christian. Daughter of James and Sarah, born
                                    March 4, 1745
Smith, Susannah. Daughter of Robert and Phillis,
                                    born April 16, 1745
Suddeth, Henry. Married Mary Latham,
                                    June 25, 1745
Suddeth, Sarah. Married Thomas Griffin,
                                    July 18, 1745

Suddeth, Ann.   Daughter of Benjamin and Silent,
                                  born July 17, 1745
Suitor, Alexander.   Married Margaret Issac,
                                  July 21, 1745
Sullivant, Mary.   Married Peter Gowing, May 28, 1745
Stacey, Catharine.   Married William Hill,
                                  September 17, 1745
Smith, George.   Son of Henry and Sarah, born
                                  October 19, 1745
Suddeth, Elizabeth.   Daughter of Lawrence and
                     Dorothy, born November 3, 1745
Simson, Elizabeth.   Daughter of Alexander and
                     Catharine, born January 4, 1746
Spoore, Ann.   Departed this life, January 29, 1746
Stark, John.   Married Howson Porter,
                                  February 1, 1746
Stark, Jeremiah.   Married Tabitha Lowry,
                                  January 29, 1747
Sayas, William.   Son of Richard and Ann, born
                                  March 10, 1747
Stone, Josias.   Son of Josias and Mary, born
                                  June 17, 1747
Sanderson, William.   Son of John and Jean, born
                                  June 7, 1747
Sims, Ann.   Married William Matheny,
                                  September 10, 1747

Smith, Martha.   Daughter of Robert, born
                        November 3, 1747
Smith, Christian.   Daughter of John and Catharine,
                        born December 2, 1747
Stark, James.   Son of James and Catharine, born
                        December 21, 1747
Simpson, Mary.   Daughter of Alexander, born
                        December 10, 1747
Smith, John.   Married Elizabeth Hornbuckle,
                        December 3, 1747
Simson, Susannah.   Daughter of George and
                        Margaret, born January 18, 1748
Suddeth, Margaret.   Daughter of Benjamin and
                        Silent, born January 12, 1748
Stark, Lydia.   Daughter of James, born June 31, 1748
Sebastian, Ann.   Married John Read, July 21, 1748
Smith, Daniel and Sarah.   Children of Henry,
                        baptized October 24, 1748
Smith, Sarah.   Daughter of Henry, died
                        October 29, 1748
Sprayburry, John.   Married Joshan Robinson,
                        November 9, 1748
Stark, John.   Son of Jeremima and Tabitha, born
                        November 6, 1748
Stacey, Silvia.   Daughter of John, Jr., born
                        December 6, 1748

Smith, Catharine.   Married Joshua Kendal,
April 4, 1749
Stone, Betty.   Daughter of Josias and Mary, born
April 14, 1749
Stacey, Mary.   Daughter of Judy and Simon, born
February 15, 1749
Sprayburry, James.   Son of John and Joshan, born
June 14, 1749
Sanderson, John.   Son of John and Jean, born
August 2, 1749
Somacks, Richard.   Died at John Peyton's, Aquia,
August 28, 1749
Stark, Elizabeth.   Daughter of John and Howson,
born August 16, 1749
Suddeth, Grace.   Daughter of Lawrence and Dorothy,
born September 23, 1749
Sturdy, Robert.   Departed this life,
November 3, 1749
Stark, Sarah Ann.   Daughter of James and Catharine,
born November 25, 1749
Stephens, Mary.   Died at Edward Balls,
January 18, 1750
Stacey, Sarah.   Married Benjamin Robinson,
January 2, 1750
Smith, Sith.   Daughter of Robert and Phillis, born
January 10, 1750

Suddeth, Catharine. Daughter of Benjamin, born
March 27, 1750

Suddeth, Catharine. Departed this life,
April 11, 1750

Spolding, Sarah. Daughter of Thomas and Sarah,
born March 4, 1750

Simpson, Jane. Daughter of John and Elizabeth,
born January 27, 1750

Smith, William. Married Betty Barbee,
January 1, 1750

Sylva, John. Married Bridget Cooper,
July 1, 1750

Smith, Enoch. Son of Henry and Sarah, born
June 21, 1750

Simms, Richard. Married Betty Bridwell,
October 15, 1750

Strother, Margaret. Married John Murdock,
October 26, 1750

Sylvy, Nancy   Daughter of John, born
October 22, 1750

Stacey, Peggy. Daughter of John and Elizabeth,
born September 14, 1750

Simpson, Sarah. Daughter of Alexander, born
December 13, 1750

Slaughter, Robert. Married Susanna Harrison,
December 11, 175C

Sinclair, George.　Died at Hannah Bailis',

January 12, 1751

Spilman, William.　Married Elizabeth Reeds,

February 25, 1751

Selden, Samuel.　Married Mary Thompson Mason,

April 11, 1751

Sinclair, Elizabeth.　Married Charles Jones,

April 21, 1751

Suddeth, William.　Son of Benjamin and Silent, born

March 7, 1751

Stone, Valentine.　Son of Josiah, baptized

April 30, 1751

Stacey, Dorothy.　Wife of John, Sr., died

February 5, 1751

Sebastian, William.　Married Sarah Kelly,

June 11, 1751

Stanard, Elizabeth.　Married William Howard,

May 29, 1751

Sanderson, Thomas.　Son of John, born

May 2, 1751

Stringfellow, Mary.　Married William Bouchard,

May 12, 1751

Spilman, Thomas.　Son of William and Elizabeth,

born November 29, 1751

Selden, Miles Carey.　Son of Samuel and Mary, born

November 28, 1751

Stark, Sarah. Daughter of Howson and John, born
January 29, 1752
Smith, Sarah. Daughter of Henry and Sarah, born
January 20, 1752
Suddeth, Lawence. Son of James and Hannah, born
February 21, 1752
Smith, Nathaniel. Son of Robert and Phillis, born
March 19, 1752
Shadborn, Frances Ann. Daughter of Jane, born
April 23, 1752
Stark, Jeremiah. Son of James, born
Jnne 11, 1752
Smith, Elizabeth. Wife of Nathaniel, died
April 25, 1752
Smith, Lydia. Married Peter Hansbrough,
May 27, 1752
Spoldin, Elizabeth. Daughter of Thomas, born
May 22, 1752
Smith, Richard. Married Susanna Davis,
November 17, 1752
Smith, Mary. Married Michael Dial,
November 19, 1752
Sturdy, William, Married Phillis Jones,
December 17, 1752
Simmons, Keziah. Married William Boning,
February 4, 1753

Sullivan, Sarah.   Married George Hinson,
                                February 4, 1753
Sanderson, Sarah.   Daughter of John, born
                                February 21, 1753
Stone, Mary.   Daughter of Josias and Mary, born
                                April 28, 1753
Sims, James.   Son of Richard, born April 16, 1753
Selden, Samuel.   Son of Samuel and Mary, born
                                March 20, 1753
Selden, Samuel.   Departed this life, April 19, 1753
Suddeth, Susannah.   Daughter of Benjamin and
                                Mary, born, April 25, 1753
Suddeth, Moses.   The son of Joseph and Jemima,
                                born July 28, 1753
Smith, Ann.   Wife of Thomas, died July 20, 1753,
                                aged 108 years
Stark, Mary.   Daughter of Tabitha and Jeremiah,
                                born May 19, 1753
Shamlin, Martha.   Married John Gunn,
                                September 30, 1758
Scoulcraft, James.   Married Margaret Mills,
                                October 14, 1753
Smith, John.   Departed this life,
                                September 23, 1753
Selman, William.   Son of Benjamin and Ann, born
                                November 19, 1753

Shoemake, Spencer. Son of William and Ann, born
November 26, 1753
Syloy, Sulky. Daughter of John and Bridget, born
February 20, 1754
Scoulcraft, Mary. Daughter of James and Margaret,
born March 11, 1754
Smith, Sarah. Daughter of Parker and Catharine,
born February 28, 1754
Stark, James. Departed this life, April 12, 1754
Sturdy, Joanna. Married Rowley Lunsford,
June 16, 1754
Stacey, Suky. Daughter of John and Elizabeth, born
July 10, 1754
Smith, Thomas. Son of Henry and Sarah, born
October 4, 1754
Smith, Margaret. Married Joseph Jeffries,
October 24, 1754
Sanderson, Jenny. Daughter of John and Jean, born
December 10, 1754
Selden, Mary Mason. Daughter of Samuel and Mary,
born October 1, 1754
Stark, William. Son of John and Howson, born
December 14, 1754
Simson, Elizabeth. Married David Bradly, Apr. 17, 1755
Spilman, Jeremiah. Married Bridget Edwards,
January 16, 1755

Smith, Susanna.　Daughter of Richard and Elizabeth,
born January 20, 1755

Stark, Howson.　Wife of John, died April 11, 1755

Sprayburry, John.　Son of John and Joshan, baptized
April 20, 1755

Smith, Rosamond.　Married William Hammet,
May 6, 1755

Skaines, Mary.　Married David Macquatty,
May 6, 1755

Stacey, Elizabeth.　Married Benjamin Robinson, Jr.,
May 25, 1755

Stacey, Peter.　Married Ruth Croscuel, May 25, 1755

Smith, Banister and Susannah Banister Smith.　Were
baptized July 6, 1755

Summers, Elizabeth.　Married John Taylor,
November 8, 1755

Simpson, Franky.　Daughter of Alexander and
Catharine, born November 13, 1755

Stone, Philadelphia.　Daughter of Mary and Josias,
born September 22, 1755

Smith, Thomas.　Married Mary Ann Williams,
February 21, 1756

Smith, Jemima.　Married Joseph Porter,
February 26, 1756

Selden, Samuel.　Son of Samuel and Mary, born
April 30, 1756

Simpson, William. Married Lettie Lunsford,

January 18, 1756

Silvy, Phobe. Daughter of John and Bridget, born

March 21, 1756

Sodarth, Sarah. Daughter of Joseph, baptized

April 13, 1756

Stacey, Shadrick. Son of John and Elizabeth, born

August 20, 1756

Shumate, William. Son of Ann and William, born

August 11, 1756

Stark, John. Married Hannah Eaves, May 29, 1756

Suddeth, Jane. Daughter of James and Hannah, born

May 18, 1756

Smith, Joseph. Son of Henry and Sarah, born

June 6, 1756

Sutherland, Dr. John. Married Susannah Brent,

September 15, 1756

Strother, Alice. Married Robert Washington,

December 16, 1756

Smith, Phillis. Married John Green,

December 19, 1756

Stark, James. Son of John and Hannah, born

February 7, 1757

Stacey, Sarah. Married Isaker Edwards, May 16, 1757

Sutor, Alexander. Married Elizabeth Raper,

May 8, 1757

Smith, John.   Married Elizabeth Welit,
                        December 7, 1757
Sumate, Lettie.   Daughter of William and Ann, born
                        February 5, 1757
Suddeth, Priscilla.   Was baptized October 23, 1757
Smith, Sarah.   Daughter of John, born
                        January 24, 1758
Smith, Mary.   Married James Hardage Lane,
                        January 12, 1758
Selden, Mary.   Wife of Samuel, Departed this life,
                        January 5, 1758
Smith, William.   Son of Thomas and Mary Ann,
                        born January 24, 1758
Simpson, Sarah.   Daughter of William and Lettie,
                        born June 25, 1758

T.

Turner, Margaret.   Daughter of Henry and Mary,
                        born June 1, 1733
Turner, Betty.   Daughter of Henry and Mary, born
                        May 28, 1736
Traverse, Peter Daniel.   Married ———
Traverse, Sarah.   Married Peter Daniel, July 15, 1736
Tyler, Margaret.   Married William Waugh,
                        September 10, 1738
Taylor, Catharine.   Married William Chimp,
                        January 31, 1739

Taylor, Elizabeth. Daughter of Henry, born
                              July 25, 1740
Trewick, Eleanor. Daughter of Robert, died
                      May 19, 1740, aged 8 years
Tunnel, Francis. Married Margaret Sinclair,
                              November 9, 1740
Trewick, Elizabeth. Daughter of Robert and
                      Marjory, born December 24, 1740
Toby, Mary. Married John Nelson,
                              February 10, 1740
Tolson, Judith. Married Simon Stacey,
                              August 22, 1741
Turner, Alexander. Son of Edward and Jean, born
                              July 25, 1741
Tunnel, Joseph. Son of Francis and Margaret, born
                              February 18, 1742
Thompson, Robert. Married Catharine Tomlinson,
                              September 1, 1742
Tomlinson, Catharine. Married Robert Thompson,
                              September 1, 1742
Turner, Hannah. Daughter of Henry and Mary,
                          born October 30, 1742
Trewick, Eleanor. Daughter of Robert and Marjory,
                          born January 24, 1743
Tyler, John. Son of Henry and Else, born
                              April 17, 1743

Tomison, Richard and William.   Sons of Simon
                            and Barbara, born August 21, 1743
Tyler Frances.   Married Anne Strother, May 17, 1744
Taylor, John.   Son of John and Eleanor, born
                            December 1, 1745
Turner, Sarah.   Departed this life, December 25, 1744
Tomison, Jane.   Daughter of Simon and Barbara,
                            born November 17, 1745
Thornberry, William.   Married Elizabeth O'Daneal,
                            July 10, 1746
Todd, Hayward.   Married Sarah Rosser,
                            September 7, 1746
Turner, Thomas.   Married Eleanor Radcliffe,
                            September 13, 1746
Thornberry, Ann.   Daughter of William and
                            Elizabeth, born April 9, 1747
Tolson, Mary.   The wife of Benjamin, died
                            June 24, 1748
Thomson, Mary.   Married Robert Pully,
                            August 28, 1748
Tomison, James.   Son of Simon and Barbara, born
                            July 8, 1748
Tomison, Elizabeth.   Daughter of Simon, died
                            September 8, 1748
Tomison, Jean.   Departed this life,
                            September 14, 1748

Threlkeld, Henry. Married Mary Hinson,
                              November 2, 1748
Tyler, Anne. Daughter of Henry and Else, baptized
                              January 30, 1749
Turnham, John. Son of Thomas and Eleanor, born
                              May 3, 1749
Traverse, Rawleigh. Departed this life,
                              October 15, 1749
Towngate, Hannah. Was born in Prince William
                              County, January 9, 1750
Tifer, Jannet. Died at Morris Lynaugh's,
                              May 9, 1750
Toby, Thomas. Son of John and Elizabeth, born
                              January 20, 1751
Tongate, Jeremiah. Married Elizabeth Waus,
                              March 3, 1751
Tyler, Mary. Daughter of Henry and Alice, baptized
                              March 20, 1751
Tomison, Barbara. Wife of Simon, died
                              August 19, 1751
Tolson, Benjamin, Jr. Married Hannah
                              Maccothough, December 31, 1751
Todd, Nanny. Daughter of William and Margaret,
                              born October 13, 1752
Todd, William. Married Margaret Cocklen,
                              October 23, 1752

Tolson, Mary.   Daughter of Benjamin and Hannah,
                        born February 19, 1753
Thomson, John Clement.   Son of Jean, born
                        February 13, 1753
Toby, John.   Son of John, born July 3, 1753
Toby, John.   Son of John, died, February 3, 1754
Tolson, Ann.   Married Isaac Dunnaway,
                        May 25, 1754
Turner, Betty.   Married Henry Dawson,
                        December 15, 1754
Ticer, William.   Married Aggy Hutt,
                        December 15, 1754
Toby, Mary.   Daughter of John and Elizabeth, born
                        July 28, 1755
Tolson, Peggy.   Was baptized September 2, 1755
Taylor, John.   Married Elizabeth Summers,
                        November 8, 1755
Taylor, Alexander.   Married Hannah Brooke,
                        February 24, 1757
Taylor, Philadelphia.   Daughter of John, born
                        February 2, 1757
Turner, James.   Married Mary Matthews,
                        March 3, 1757
Thomas, Jane.   Married Feanly McCoy, July 18, 1757
Tolson, Nanny.   Daughter of Benjamin and Hannah,
                        born December 4, 1757

U.

V.

Voucheart, John. Son of William, born
October 21, 1752
Voucheart, John. Was baptized December 10, 1752
Vant, Franky. Daughter of James and Margaret, born
May 15, 1758

W.

Williams, Nathaniel. Son of George and Jean, born
October 5, 1730.
Williams, Margaret. Daughter of George and Jean,
born April 17, 1732
Williams, Benjamin. Son of George and Jean, born
June 14, 1734
Wright, John. Son of William and Rosamond, born
August 3, 1735
Williams, George. Son of George and Jean, born
August 21, 1736
Wright, Betty. Daughter of William and Rosamond,
born September 10, 1737
Wine, Richard. Married Anne Harvie, July 23, 1738

Waugh, William. Married Margaret Tyler,
September 10, 1738
Wells, Carty. Married Elizabeth Onsby,
September 28, 1738
Waters, Thomas. Married Catharine Hays,
September 28, 1738
Waters, Margaret. Daughter of Edward and
Catharine, January 25, 1739
Waugh, Tyler. Son of William and Margaret, born
February 29, 1739
Waters, Philmen. Son of Thomas, born
March 22, 1739
Williams, John Pope. Son of George and Jean, born
July 27, 1739
Whealy, James. Married Hannah Higgerson,
July 8, 1739
Whitecotton, Mary. Daughter of George and
Bridget, born January 20, 1739
Whitson, Margaret. Married Nicholas George,
December 25, 1740
Whitson, William. Son of William and Margaret,
born March 11, 1741
Wright, Constance. Daughter of William and
Rosamond, September 7, 1739
Welch, Margaret. Married John Prim,
September 9, 1739

Wells, Sarah. Daughter of Carty and Elizabeth, born
October 10, 1739
Waters, James. Son of Thomas and Mary, born
October 25, 1739
Waller, Hannah. Daughter of George and Elizabeth,
born October 12, 1739
Wells, Charles. Son of Charles and Mary, born
January 10, 1740
Waugh, Elizabeth. Daughter of Joseph and Millon,
born March 31, 1740
Waugh. Mary. Married Alexander Doniphon,
June 17, 1740
Williams, Mary. Died at Charles Turner's,
June 20, 1740
Waugh, James. Married Betty French,
August 22, 1740
Wilkinson, William. Married Sarah Heffermot,
August 21, 1740
Wine, Mary. Daughter of Richard and Anne, born
October 1, 1740
Waller, William. Son of Edward and Anne, born
November 26, 1740
Wiot, Edmond. Son of Daniel and Susannah, born
October 1, 1740
Williams, Joseph. Married Mary Mallaken,
February 9, 1741

Withers, Elizabeth.   Daughter of John and Hannah,
                              born February 8, 1741
Wood, Archibald.   Son of John and Tabitha, born
                              April 15, 1741
Wells, Sarah.   Daughter of Carty, died April 13, 1741
Wilkinson, John.   Son of William, born July 6, 1741
Waugh, John.   Son of James and Betty, born
                              October 20, 1741
Wells, Isabel.   Daughter of Carty and Elizabeth, born
                              October 31, 1741
Waugh, Priscilla.   Daughter of William and
                              Margaret, born October 22, 1741
Waller, Margaret.   Daughter of Charles and
                              Elizabeth, born November 27, 1741
Whitecotton, Lettie and Jean.   Daughters of Sarah,
                              born November 14, 1741
Wiot, William.   Son of Edmund and ———, born
                              November 20, 1741
Williams, Jesse.   Son of George and Jean, born
                              December 21, 1741
Wade, Rachel.   Married John McGuirk,
                              December 25, 1741
Webster, Edmund.   Married Margery Stanley,
                              November 20, 1741
Whitson, William.   Son of Samuel and Nan, born
                              January 29, 1742

Williams, George. Son of Joseph, born
January 19, 1742

Waller, John. Son of Edward and Anne, born
April 7, 1742

Whitson, Charles. Son of William and Margaret,
born March 5, 1742

Watson, Andrew. Married Mary Moses,
September 26, 1742

Wright, Windfield. Son of William and Rose, born
March 22, 1742

Waters, Anne. Daughter of Edward and Catharine,
born January 1, 1742

Wells, John. Son of Charles and Mary, born
July 3, 1742

West, James. Son of John, born September 26, 1742

Wine, Benjamin. Son of Richard and Anne, born
December 19, 1742

Warner, Margaret. Married James Dillon,
November 6, 1742

Wise, John. Son of John and Mary, born
October 6, 1742

Wise, Elizabeth. Married Patrick Roath,
October 9, 1742

Waugh, John. Departed this life, November 17, 1742

Waugh, Traverse. Son of Joseph William, born
January 24, 1743

Withers, Bridget. Married William Allen,
                              February 15, 1743
Withers, Margaret. Daughter of John and Hannah,
                              born February 8, 1743
Webster, Anne. Married George Reaves, April 3, 1743
West, Carty. Daughter of Thomas and Catharine,
                              born March 12, 1743
Watson, John. Son of Elizabeth, born
                              January 27, 1743
Waters, Mary. Married John Shaw, June 12, 1743
Waters, John. Married Elizabeth Higgerson,
                              June 3, 1743
White, George. Married Anne Doniphan,
                              August 4, 1743
Wells, George. Son of Carty and Elizabeth, born
                              November 18, 1743
Whitcomb, John. Married Elizabeth Simpson,
                              November 24, 1743
Whitson, James. Son of William and Margaret, born
                              February 10, 1744
Whitson, Mary. Daughter of Samuel and Ann, born
                              April 19, 1744
Whitecotton, George. Departed this life,
                              March 23, 1744
Want, Sarah. Married William Corbin,
                              August 2, 1744

Whitcomb, Mary. Daughter of John, born
August 29, 1744

Withers, Wilmouth. Died at William Mathews,
August 21, 1744

Waller, Margaret. Daughter of George, born
July 27, 1744

Waugh, Sarah. Daughter of Betty and James,
baptized June 20, 1744

Walker, William. Married Elizabeth Monk,
May 23, 1744

Wells, Peyton. Son of Charles, born
Sepember 9, 1744

Withers, Ann. Married Henry Manzey,
November 11, 1744

Whitson, Elizabeth. Married George Green,
December 23, 1744

Whitson, Mary. Departed this life, January 25, 1745

Withers, Mary. Daughter of John and Hannah, born
January 22, 1745

Waters, Edward. Departed this life, February 2, 1745

West, Dorothy. Married Lawrence Suddeth,
April 18, 1745

Wine, Richard. Son of Richard and Ann, born
February 14, 1745

Wilkerson, John. Son of William, died
March 10, 1745

Williams, Charles.   Son of George and Jane, born
May 1, 1745

Whitson, Sarah.   Married John Nelson,
December 7, 1745

Whalebone, Duke.   Married Elizabeth Powell,
December 3, 1745

Whitson, Mary   Married William George,
November 1, 1745

Wood, Ann.   Daughter of Thomas and Margaret,
born September 18, 1745

Waller, Charles.   Son of Edward and Ann, born
January 27, 1746

Williams, Margaret.   Married John Ball,
January 2, 1746

Waugh, James.   Son of James and Elizabeth, born
February 4, 1746

West, James.   Son of Thomas and Catharine, born
February 10, 1746

Whitcomb, Richard.   Departed this life,
February 7, 1746

Withers, James.   Departed this life in the 66th year of
his age, June 3, 1746

Whitson, Ann.   Daughter of Ann, born June 17, 1746

Wheeler, John.   Departed this life, August 5, 1746

Waller, Jeany.   Daughter of George and Elizabeth,
born July 28, 1746

Wise, Samuel. Son of John, born July 15, 1746

Waller, Elizabeth. Was baptized September 7, 1746

Waugh, James. Son of James and Betty, died
September 3, 1746

Whalebone, Thomas. Son of Duke and Elizabeth,
born September 4, 1746

Wiggonton, Peter. Married Winefred Eaves,
October 13, 1746

Weeks, Anny. Married Edward Proctor,
February 15, 1747

Wells, Eleanor. Daughter of Charles, born
April 19, 1747

Walker, Elizabeth. Daughter of William and
Elizabeth, born April 3, 1747

Withers, William. Son of John and Hannah, born
March 21, 1747

Wiggonton, Anne. Died at home,
November 22, 1747

Waugh, Betty. Daughter of James and Betty, born
September 4, 1747

Waugh, Betty. Departed this life,
September 14, 1747

Waters, Diana. Daughter of Thomas and Mary, born
November 5, 1747

Whitecotton, Bridget. Married William McConchie,
November 10, 1747

White, Mary.   Daughter of George and Ann, born
September 9, 1747

White, Rosamond.   Departed this life,
February 19, 1748

Wright, Jane.   Married Richard Nowland,
December 26, 1747

Withers, Keene.   Married Elizabeth Cave,
December 21, 1747

Waugh, Joseph.   Died September 4, 1747

Wine, Richard.   Had two children born September 2,
1747, one of them died September 28, 1748

Weddall, Thomas.   Married Isabel Robe,
January, 3, 1748

White, Rosamond.   Departed this life,
February 19, 1748

Waller, Ann.   Wife of Edward, died February 29, 1748

Waller, Edward.   Son of Edward, born
February 27, 1748

Weathers, Susannah.   Daughter of John and Judy,
born February 1, 1748

Whitecotton, Axton.   Son of Husband Foot, born
February 3, 1748

Wood, Lizzie.   Daughter of Thomas and Margaret,
born March 18, 1748

Waugh, Solomon.   Married Betty Chinn,
April 13, 1748

Waters, Diana,   Daughter of Thomas, died
                                    May 27, 1748
Waller, John.   Son of Edward, died June 6, 1748
Waller, Susannah.   Departed this life,
                                    October 18, 1748
Wilson, John.   Married Ann Asberry, August 16, 1748
Weathers, Susannah.   Daughter of Judy, died
                                    October 9, 1748
Waters, Jean.   Married John Monslow,
                                    October 26, 1748
Withers, Ann.   Daughter of Cain and Betty, baptized
                                    December 4, 1748
Wingfield, Owen.   Married Mary Hurst,
                                    November 26, 1748
Wood, Lizzie.   Daughter of Thomas and Margaret,
                                    died November 13, 1748
Waugh, Mieajiah.   Son of Solomon and Elizabeth,
                                    born January 9, 1749
Withers, Thomas.   Son of John and Hannah, born
                                    January 15, 1749
Williams, William.   Son of Jean, born
                                    January 26, 1749
White, Joseph.   Married Elizabeth Gill,
                                    January 31, 1749
Webster, Barbara.   Married William Groves,
                                    February 2, 1749

Wiggonton, William.   Son of Peter and Winefred,
born May 29, 1749

Whitcomb, Margaret.   Daughter of John and
Elizabeth, born August 16, 1749

Weathers, Nancy.   Daughter of John and Judith,
born July 1, 1749

Whitcomb, Mary.   Died at Richard Wine's,
April 23, 1751

Whalebone, Nanny.   Daughter of Duke and
Elizabeth, born October 5, 1749

White, Alice.   Daughter of Joseph and Elizabeth,
born December 18, 1749

Weathers, Ann.   Daughter of Ann and Thomas, born
December 10, 1749

Wine, Peggy.   Daughter of Richard and Ann, born
December 2, 1749

Waller, Charles.   Died at John Waugh's,
December 4, 1749

Walker, Mary.   Daughter of William and Elizabeth,
born January 9, 1750

Wilson, Ann.   Died at John Dayton's,
December 31, 1749

Wiggonton, Jane.   Married Moses Bland,
January 14, 1750

Wells, Eleanor.   Daughter of Carty, born
February 21, 1750

Williams, George. Departed this life,
February 12, 1750
Wilson, Mary, Died at William Lunsford's,
March 9, 1750
Wood, Thomas. Departed this life, February 8, 1750
Whitson, Jess. Son of William and Margaret, born
May 8, 1750
Wood, Elizabeth. Daughter of Thomas and Margaret,
born April 29, 1750
Waugh, Captain James. Departed this life,
May 9, 1750
Weathers, Samuel. Departed this life, June 30, 1750
Wawal, Charles. Married Mary Hall,
November 16, 1751
Weathers, Elizabeth Blufard. Mother of Thomas,
died August 13, 1750
Wilson, Spencer. Son of John and Ann, born
August 30, 1750
White, Alexander. Son of George and Ann, born
August 11, 1750
Waters, William. Married Jean Cash, April 6, 1751
Wiggonton, Henry. Married Margaret Bridwell,
November 12, 1750
Wans, Elizabeth. Married Jeremiah Lungate,
March 3, 1751
Waller, John. Married Mary Mathews, July 4, 1751

Waller, Ann.   Married Thomas Bailly,
                                    July 10, 1751
Waugh, Betty.   Married Andrew Edwards,
                                    May 7, 1751
Wells, Benjamin.   Son of Charles and Mary, born
                                    August 22, 1751
Whitson, Elizabeth.   Married Benjamin
                        MacCollough, December 17, 1751
Waller, William.   Son of John and Mary, born
                                    December 24, 1751
Waller, Elizabeth.   Married John Peyton,
                                    November 17, 1751
Winlock, Elizabeth.   Daughter of Joseph and
                        Margaret, born April 12, 1752
Whitcomb, Eliza.   Daughter of John, born
                                    February 26, 1752
Wilson, Nanny.   Daughter of John, born
                                    February 25, 1752
Wilson, John.   Married Sarah Brooks,
                                    February 7, 1752
Weathers, John.   Son of John and Judith, born
                                    March 14, 1752
Waters, Mary.   Married John Fitzpatrick,
                                    February 12, 1752
Washington, William.   Son of Baily and Catharine,
                            born February 28, 1752

Weathers, Joel. Son of Thomas and Ann, born
February 7, 1752
Walker, Margaret. Daughter of William and
Elizabeth, baptized May 1, 1752
Withers, James. Son of Keene, born May 9, 1752
Wiggonton, Peter. Son of Peter and Winney, born
September 17, 1752
West, Edward. Married Elizabeth Mills,
October 6, 1752
Waller, Mary. Married Edward Kendon,
April 15, 1753
Wren, James. Married Catharine Brent,
March 27, 1753
Wright, Rosamond. Wife of William, died
March 16, 1753
Waugh, David. Died at Priscilla Hayes',
March 22, 1753
Withers, George. Son of John and Hannah, born
February 2, 1753
White, Thomas. Was baptized May 3, 1753
Waller, Theodosia. Daughter of George, baptized
April 1, 1753
Waters, Jean. Daughter of Charles and Hannah,
born June 28, 1753
Wilson, Hannah. Daughter of John, born
June 16, 1753

Waller, Sarah. Daughter of John and Mary, born
June 12, 1753
Waller, Edward. Departed this life suddenly,
November 20, 1753
Washington, Bailey. Son af Bailey, born
December 12, 1753
Wright, William. Married Mary Brent,
October 18, 1753
White, Ann. Daughter of Ann and George, born
January 14, 1754
Withers, William. Son of Keene and Elizabeth,
February 20, 1754
Williams, Elizabeth. Married John Gill,
March 3, 1754
Waters, James. Son of William and Jane, born
May 26, 1754
White, Alice. Daughter of Joseph and Elizabeth,
died August 13, 1754
Waller, Mary. Married George Dabney,
September 11, 1754
Withers, Hannah. Daughter of John and Hannah,
born September 8, 1754
Waller, Milly. Daughter of Charles, died
January 7, 1755
Winlock, Sarah. Daughter of Joseph and Margaret,
born February 10, 1755

West, William Mills. Son of Edward and Elizabeth,
                                    born March 29, 1755
Wilson, John. Son of John and Ann, born
                                    March 25, 1755
Woodward, Jenny. Daughter of William and
                            Hannah, born August 10, 1755
Wilson, Else. Daughter of John and Ann, born
                                    May 16, 1757
Wren, James. Son of Catharine, baptized
                                    December 21, 1758
Waller, Edward. Son of John and Mary, born
                                    December 10, 1755
Wiggonton, James. Son of Peter and Winefred, died
                                    February 10, 1755
Withers, John. Son of Cain, born
                                    February 23, 1756
Williams, Mary Ann. Married Thomas Smith,
                                    February 21, 1756
Wheeler, Eleanor. Married William Edwards,
                                    February 12, 1756
Wiggonton, James. Married Sarah Botts,
                                    February 9, 1756
Wheeler, Martha. Married William Howard,
                                    April 25, 1756
Withers, Mary Ann. Daughter of Thomas and Ann,
                                    born, April 19, 1756

Washington, John.   Son of Bailey and Catharine,
                                    born May 5, 1756
Wiggonton, Nancy.   Daughter of James and Sarah,
                                    born November 8, 1756
Waters, Mark.   Married Ann Harding, July 20, 1756
Washington, Robert.   Married Alice Strother,
                                    December 16, 1756
Willamson, James.   Married Susannah Weyton,
                                    November 4, 1756
Withers, Ann.   Daughter of John and Hannah, born
                                    November 9, 1756
Weyton, Susannah.   Married James Williamson,
                                    November 4, 1756
Wall, Margaret.   A poor parisioner, died
                                    April 7, 1757
Waters, Virginia.   Married Richard Fristoe,
                                    February 28, 1757
Wiggonton, James.   Son of Peter and Winney, born
                                    February 24, 1757
Weathers, Eleanor.   Daughter of John and Judith,
                                    born January 15, 1757
Wilson, Else.   Was baptized August 25, 1757
Withers, James.   Married Sukey Waller,
                                    December 7, 1757
Waller, Sukey.   Married James Withers,
                                    December 7, 1757

Welit, Elizabeth.   Married John Smith,
                                      December 7, 1757
White, Ann.   Died at Edward Templeman's,
                                      December 13, 1757
Weathers, Ann.   Wife of Thomas, died
                                      October 13, 1757
Weathers, Jean and Ann.   Daughters of Thomas and
                          Ann, born October 13, 1757
Winlock, Joseph.   Son of Joseph and Margaret, born
                                      May 11, 1758
Washington, Elizabeth.   Daughter of Catharine and
                          Bailey, born March 16, 1758
Withers, Elizabeth.   Married Andrew Edwards,
                                      January 19, 1758
Waller, John.   Son of John and Mary, born
                                      December 27, 1758

X.

Y.

Young, Margaret.   Married John Humphreys, Jr.,
                                      September 23, 1738
Young, William.   Married Patience Sinclair,
                                      July 23, 1744

Young, Robert. Son of William and Patience, born
May 30, 1745

Young, Robert. Son of William, died
October 1, 1745

Yelton, James. Married Isabell Hinson,
November 13, 1743

Yelton, Charles. Son of James and Isabell, born
November 1, 1746

Young, Richard. Married Elizabeth Green,
December 27, 1746

Young, Sarah. Daughter of William and Patience,
born April 1, 1747

Yelton, James. Son of James and Isabell, born
July 15, 1749

Young, John. Departed this life at William Kirke's
March 11, 1752

Yelton, Mary. Daughter of James and Isabell, born
April 18, 1752

Yelton, Ann. Daughter of James and Isabell, born
July 26, 1755

Yates, Elizabeth. Married ———, February 4, 1758

Z.

This Register was brought to William Moncure's residence in the year 1825 by his son, William R. Moncure, who was a great grandson of the Rev. John Moncure, Minister of Overwharton Parish, and was recently found among the papers of Judge R. C. L. Moncure, by his executor, Powhatan Moncure, Stafford County, Virginia, and by me copied for Mr. Wm. F. Boogher, of Washington, D. C., and I hereby certify that from pages 1 to 194, inclusive, of this book contains a true copy, (including spelling,) of the Register of Overwharton Parish, Stafford County, Virginia, from 1720 to 1758 omitting only such items as refers to negroes.

POWHATAN MONCURE,

Custodian of Old Records of said Parish.

October 10, 1899.